WORLD POLITICAL ORDER

AN ANALYSIS

Y V ANAND SAGAR

Copyright © Y V Anand Sagar
All Rights Reserved.

This book has been self-published with all reasonable efforts taken to make the material error-free by the author. No part of this book shall be used, reproduced in any manner whatsoever without written permission from the author, except in the case of brief quotations embodied in critical articles and reviews.

The Author of this book is solely responsible and liable for its content including but not limited to the views, representations, descriptions, statements, information, opinions and references ["Content"]. The Content of this book shall not constitute or be construed or deemed to reflect the opinion or expression of the Publisher or Editor. Neither the Publisher nor Editor endorse or approve the Content of this book or guarantee the reliability, accuracy or completeness of the Content published herein and do not make any representations or warranties of any kind, express or implied, including but not limited to the implied warranties of merchantability, fitness for a particular purpose. The Publisher and Editor shall not be liable whatsoever for any errors, omissions, whether such errors or omissions result from negligence, accident, or any other cause or claims for loss or damages of any kind, including without limitation, indirect or consequential loss or damage arising out of use, inability to use, or about the reliability, accuracy or sufficiency of the information contained in this book.

Made with ♥ on the Notion Press Platform
www.notionpress.com

I dedicate this book to my family, my mother Y.Vijayalakshmi, my late father Y.V.K.Sastry, my brother Y.V.Shanti Swarup, my sister Y.L.Saroja and Nalini Varanasi, my Editor, without whose tireless efforts this work would never have been possible. A special word of thanks is in order for my teachers who made me what I am today.

Contents

Foreword *vii*

World Political Order-An Analysis *ix*

   1. The Big Five   1

   2. Jewel Of Asia   52

   3. Western Europe   57

   4. Eastern Europe   77

   5. South East Asia   85

   6. South Asia   95

   7. West Asia(or Middle East As The British Like To Call It)   120

   8. Central Asia   135

   9. Australia And Others   139

World Political Order-II

   10. Africa-The Dark Continent   147

   11. South America-the Presidential Continent   166

   12. Central America   170

   13. North America   184

Foreword

Y. V. Anand Sagar

The Author of the Book **World Political Order** is a journalist and writer. He holds a **B.Com** from **IGNOU** and a **P-G Diploma in Mass Communications from Bharatiya Vidya Bhavan, Bangalore.** He is a member of the **Karnataka Journalists Union** which is affliated to the **Indian Federation of Working Journalists, the largest of its kind in the Non-Aligned World** and is a **Fellow of the United Writers Association, Chennai.** He is well versed in niche and high pressure fields like Foreign Affairs, Defense, Home Affairs, Regional Affairs, Business, Science and has some sports knowledge too. He has done extreme, extensive and exhaustive research on the Net delving, diving and sifting through thousands of databases steadily imbibing and ingraining knowledge in to his psyche spread across a lifetime. He has a passion for knowledge and his passion for knowledge extends to the Multimedia too. **As a value addition he has done a German A1 Course securing 81%, A Grade and the next senior level A2 securing 78%, B Grade. He has also done a Course in Office Automation securing first class in software and distinction in hardware. To boot he has won prizes including 1st and 2nd Prizes in Quiz Competitions and participated in Essay competitions. He has also won prizes in Quiz competions at school level.**

WORLD POLITICAL ORDER-AN ANALYSIS

Executive Summary

The Book **World Political Order** draws on the contours of the power architecture of the Big-5 and other countries dealing in depth with the politics of each power center even as new power centers emerge. Will the traditional power trolley be kicked down the blind alley by the new power centers? The Book also discusses at some length the role of the Big-5 in various flashpoints around the globe. What is the new common enemy? Will the world succeed in vanquishing it? Read on...

1

The Big Five

The United States

Hemispherical Political Models which characterized the world under the Obama machine did areceding act under the Trump juggernaut with a slant towards a unipolar world. Former U.S. President Donald Trump went full steam ahead with his America-First policy [witness the tit for tat tariff war that took place between the United States and China where the United States imposed tariffs on 818 Chinese items and China imposed return tariffs on American soyabeans (which hit Trump's base-American Mid-West farmers in states like Iowa etc) and lobsters , a favorite of the Chinese palate] which made China open a lifeline with countries like India and Germany (for e.g. China expressed interest in the Germany 4.0 model) Incidentally, this move by America prompted American experts to warn that such steps posed downside risks to the American economy. However, more recent reports showed that such unilateral action by America worked against Russia, China, and Iran worked but with a caveat that America should not abuse it. Also, America imposed tariffs on Indian steel and aluminium with India retaliating by imposing tariffs on 29 American items. It is transition time in the United States and the new American

President Joseph Robinette Joe Biden who was born in the rust belt town of Scranton, Pennsylvania on 20th November, 1942 and who turned 79 recently and who metamorphosised from the youngest US Senator to the oldest American President(he pipped Reagan in the bud), could return to the multipolar, " consensus" based approach of the previous Obama administration[while all but is lost for Trump{for whom calming a crying baby was just one more ball in the air to juggle when he hit the campaign trail in 2016(an election gimmick? Perhaps, but such 'tear-jerkers' have their pull among the emotional and are the laundry and bucket list of things to do for politicians, at least in the United States. It is the staple diet of politicians in the United States as they try to wean away the electorate from the opposition, but only in the right admixture. There should be no overkill.)} it is worth remembering that there is at least one American President, Grover Cleveland, who served non-consecutive terms as the 22nd and the 24th American President. But Trump is no Cleveland and it would be a real Sisyphean and uphill task for him to make a future grab for the hot seat with a hostile media in tow and it is really difficult to conjure up visions of him doing a Cleveland. Indeed, an effort was made to bring in a law to prevent him from doing just that. But, it came a cropper.] as he is a "Blue" i.e. a Democrat like Obama.

The American Power Architecture

Coming to the American power architecture under Trump, the Secretary of State was Mike Pompeo who was the 71st American Secretary of State [(and a former C.I.A. Director), American officials included Secretary of Defense Mark Thomas Esper (a former Army Secretary who served in the U. S. Army's 102 Airborne Division during the Gulf War of 1991) [former Secretaries of Defense include first James Vincent Forrestal, Marine Corps General James ' Mad Dog' Mattis, Jim Mattis, a former CENTCOM(Central Command) Commander with oversight over Iraq and Afghanistan, Cordell Hull during the time of Japanese emperor Konoe, the famous George C.

Marshall of Marshall Plan fame under which America transferred nearly $15 Billion in aid to the war ravaged economies of Europe after World War 2, notably Germany, Japan and France, Caspar 'Cap' Weinberger during the Jimmy Carter era, who incidentally served the longest as Defense Secretary, a total of seven years, Robert McNamara during the Vietnam War, Sandra Day O'Connor during the Clinton era, Robert Gates in the first year of President Barack Obama's presidency, Leon Panetta during Barack Obama's first term, Ashton Carter during Barack Obama's second term and others].

The new American Secretary of State under President Joe Biden is Antony Blinken and the new American Secretary of Defense is Llyod James Austin III, a former CENTCOM (Central Command) Commander. Former Federal Reserves Chairperson Janet Yellen is the new Secretary of the Treasury while Deb Haaland is the new Secretary of the Interior. Merrick Garland is the Attorney General while Xavier Beccerra is the new Secretary of Health and Human Services even as Nicholas Cochhran serves as the Acting Secretary of Health and Human Services as Xavier Beccerra undergoes Senate confirmation. Meanwhile, the Senate has confirmed Xavier Beccerra and Mr. Beccerra has since taken over as the new Secretary of Health and Human Services. The new Commerce Secretary is former Rhode Island Governor Gina Marie Raimondo, a venture capitalist by profession, and as Miss Raimondo moves to Capitol Hill as the new Commerce Secretary Lt.Governor Daniel Dan Mckee has taken over as the new Rhode Island Governor. The new Agriculture Secretary is Tom Vilsack while Martin Marty Walsh will be sworn in as the new Secretary of Labor once he undergoes Senate confirmation. Till then, Al Stewart will function as the Acting Secretary of Labor. Marty Walsh has since taken over as the Secretary of Labor. The new Secretary of Transportation is former Presidential candidate Pete Butigieg and the new Secretary of Energy is Hollywood icon, Jennifer Granholm while Marcia Fudge, a black, replaces Ben Carson as the Secretary of Housing and Urban Development adding color to the cabinet. The new Secretary of

Veteran Affairs is Dan Doughnoughton and the new Secretary of Homeland Security is Alejandro Mayorkas. These are all the Cabinet-level appointments. Coming to the Executive Department-level Heads in the Biden administration Ron Klain replaces Reince Priebus as the White House Chief of Staff as Steven Kevin Steve Bannon position as the Chief Strategist is left unfilled. While Katherine Tai has been appointed U.S. Trade Representative, Avril Haines is the U.S. Director of National Intelligence with oversight over the U.S. Intelligence Community as Michael. S. Regan has been appointed as the Administrator of the U.S. Environmental Protection Agency with prospects of America (it was the last country holding out) again joining the Paris Climate Agreement under the liberal administration of President Biden. He succeeds Scott Priut, a climate sceptic who was appointed by Donald Trump, himself a climate sceptic under whom America pulled out of the Paris Climate Agreement. Isabel Guzman is the new Administrator for Small Business Administration while Neera Tandon, an Indian American is the Director of the Office of Management and Budget. Linda Thomas Greenfield succeeds Kelly Knight Kraft (a former ambassador to Canada) as America's United Nations Ambassador. Former Presidential candidate John Kerry is Presidential Special Envoy for Climate while Eric Lander is the President's Science Advisor and Director of the Office of Science and Technology. These are all the Executive Department-Level Heads. It is noteworthy that a few new Cabinet positions have been created for the first time. They were not there under previous administrations. Coming to the Agency heads and other positions the new NSA or National Security Advisor is Jake Sullivan while the new CIA Director is former Ambassador to Russia, William Joseph Burns. However, Mr. Burns has to undergo Senate confirmation. Till then David Cohen is the acting CIA Director. Mr. Burns has since taken over as CIA Director. Mr. Joe Biden has decided to retain Christopher Wray as the FBI Director. Brian Deese has been appointed as the Director of the National Economic Council succeeding Larry Kudlow. India's Bharat Ramurthi is the Deputy Director. Other Directors include

Jeffrey Zients and others. Kate Bedingfield is the White House Communications Director or White House Director of Strategic Communications. As Lisa Monaco awaits Senate confirmation, John.P.Carlin serves as the Acting Deputy Attorney General. Miss Monaco has since taken over as the Deputy Attorney General. Babette Boelick is the Deputy Assistant Attorney General. As India's Vanita Gupta awaits Senate confirmation, Michael Colangelo is the Acting Associate Attorney General. Miss Gupta has since taken over as the Associate Attorney General and Elizabeth Prelogar is the Solicitor General. These are all the new appointments under President Joe Biden. The first Secretary of the Interior(not to be confused with Minister of Interior in other countries, a position which is equal to a combination of the Secretary of Homeland Security and Attorney General in America with the Secretary of the Interior, who has oversight over Disaster Management and Natural Resources playing a rather subordinate role in America than the Minister of the Interior in other countries) under Trump was Ryan Zincke (first ever Secretary of the Interior of America is Thomas. E. Ewing), and David Bernhadt succeeded him in that position, Secretary of the Treasury was Steven Mnuchin (former Secretaries of the Treasury include the first Alexander Hamilton' Ank' Henry Polson, Paul H. O'Niel who left the administration in a huff after a public spat with the administration of George Bush Jr. and others.) , Secretary of Urban Development was Ben Carson, an African-American neurosurgeon who contested the 2016 Presidential election which saw Trump becoming President, but was later inducted into the cabinet by Donald Trump, Secretary of Commerce Wilbur Ross(31st American President Herbert Hoover who passed away in the upscale Waldorf Astoria hotel in New York of a heart attack was Secretary of Commerce before he became President), Secretary of Energy (A Department which is important in the United States as the Nuclear Regulatory Establishment which oversees America's nuclear weapons and nuclear activities comes under it) was Dan Brouilette of Texas, preceded by Rick Perry (a former Texas Governor), both under Trump(incidentally, noted

Indian American nuclear expert Rita Barnwal was the Assistant Secretary of Energy). The first American Secretary of Energy was James Scheslinger who was also the Chairman of the now defunct American Atomic Energy Agency and who was also the only Secretary of Energy to be appointed by Democratic President Jimmy Carter and Republican President Ronald Reagan but he did not survive the job as politics played spoilsport with his career, the first female Secretary of Energy was Clinton's first Hazel O'Leary who was also the first African-American to hold the job, the first Hispanic Secretary of Energy was Clinton's second Federico Pena of Colorado, a former Denver Mayor and South Carolina Governor, the first Arab Secretary of Energy was Abraham Spencer appointed by the Republican administration of George Walker Bush and the first Asian Secretary of Energy was Nobel Chemistry Laureate Steven Chu, an international authority on fusion, appointed by Barack Obama who however, was caught in a maze of lawsuits. However, Chu won the lawsuits and his detractors had egg on their face. Other Secretaries of Energy include Charles Duncan who followed Scheslinger, Duncan was followed by the "do nothing, say nothing" (as the American media dubbed him for his inaction and ineptness) James Edwards whose exit was met with relief by the American media. Edwards was followed by former Secretary of Transportation Donald Hodel, who in turn, was followed by the former Under Secretary of Transportation John Herrington. Other American Secretaries of Energy are James Watkins, a former Chief of Naval Operations, Bill Richardson, Samuel Bodman, Daniel Poneman of Ohio, the style icon Earnest Moniz and Grace Bochenek. The Secretary of Education under Trump was Betsy DeVos.

Alice Wells was the Assistant Secretary of State for South and Central Asia under Trump with luminaries like Robin Lynn Raphel(who is a former US Ambassador to Pakistan along with her husband Arnold Raphel) and who held important assignments in volatile flashpoints like Afghanistan and Iraq having also served as US Ambassador to Tunisia and Karl Inderfurth gracing the office before her(a former Deputy Assistant Secretary for South Asia is India's Nisha Desai Biswal who is now the President of the Indo-US Business Council). Secretary of Homeland Security was Chad Wolf (other American Secretaries of Homeland Security include first Secretary Thomas R Ridge who was appointed in the immediate aftermath of 9/11 with a brief which includes combating terrorism, an important function of the Secretary of Homeland Security apart from other functions, Acting Secretary Kevin McAleenan and Kirstjen Nielsen). U.S. Special Envoy for Afghanistan is Zalmay Khalilzad who was also U.S. Ambassador to United Nations and Iraq as also Pakistan and who is a known American hardliner towards Pakistan. Among National Security Advisors are John R. Bolton, a known hawk whose exit was met with relief in world capitals from London to Moscow and who was succeeded for a brief while by Charles Kupperman who in turn was replaced by Robert C. O'Brien (former National Security Advisors include Lt. General H. R. McMaster and Gen. Michael W. Flynn under Trump, Susan Elizabeth Ann Rice, who was also a U.S. Ambassador to U.N during the Obama years, Gen Colin L. Powell(during the Reagan era),Gen. John. M. Poindexter, Gen. Brent Snowcraft, W. Anthony Lake (during the Clinton era), Henry A. Kissinger (also a former American Secretary of State), William Harding Jackson William. H. Jackson, Gordon Gray, Dillon Anderson, Thomas 'Tom' Edward Donilon (the 23rd National Security Advisor in the Obama Administration from 2010-13 who also worked in the Carter and Clinton administration including as Chief of Staff of the U.S. State Department, Zbignew Kazimierz 'Zbig' Brezinski, a Polish-American political scientist and diplomat, who was National Security Advisor under President Jimmy Carter, the very first National Security Advisor Robert Cutler and others.

American Intelligence Agency (along with its Dirty Tricks Department) and United States Department of Justice

CIA Directors include the controversial Gina Haspel (controversial because she was accused of using waterboarding torture techniques against prisoners during the Vietnam War and about whom it was said at the time "people like her should not be allowed to hold any public office, let alone head an agency" under Donald Trump and whom Trump retained in his cabinet despite the insinuations against her and her predecessor Mike Pompeo. John Brennan was another American CIA Director. The US Justice Department is headed by the Secretary of Justice. John .F. Kennedy's brother, Robert F. Kennedy once headed the Department of Justice as Secretary of Justice and who was also the Attorney General from 1962-1967. Attorney Generals include the very first Attorney General Edmund Randolph who entered office on September 26th, 1789, first woman and first African American Attorney General Janet Reno, Mathew Whitaker, Jeff Sessions[a former Alabama Senator, who was succeeded by Democrat Douglas "Doug" Jones who created history by storming the Red Bastion(Red standing for the Republican Party) and becoming the first Democrat Alabama Senator in 25 years only to again create an even bigger history by becoming the only Democrat Senator to be defeated in Mandate 2020 by Republican Tommy Tuberville[who secured the Republican nomination defeating Jeff Sessions who had returned to Alabama politics after his tenure as American Attorney General was over. Before the 2020 Alabama Senate election, Alabama was one among nine American States to send a split Senate delegation, represented in the Senate by both Douglas 'Doug' Jones and Richard Shelby]], William'Bill' Barr, a Republican and a staunch Trump loyalist and numerous others. Attorney Generals in states include Oregon Attorney General Ellen F. Rosenblum, a former judge of the Oregon High Court, Wisconsin Attorney General Josh Kaul (an Indian American), New Jersey Attorney General Gurbir.S.Grewal who is the State's first Sikh Attorney General, Virginia Attorney General Mark Rankin Herring and others. The Deputy Attorney General under Trump was Brian C.Rabbitt preceded by Jeffrey.A. Rosen and others, the Deputy Assistant Attorney General was Rene Augustine and the acting Associate Attorney General was Claire McCusker Murray(a former Deputy Attorney General for Strategy is Dina Habib Powell, an Egyptian American who was born in Cairo(her parents are Hodi Suleiman and Onsi Habib and her husband is Richard Powell). The acting Solicitor General was Jeff Wall, preceded by Noel John Francisco and the first Solicitor General was Benjamin .J. Bristow. A former Deputy Attorney General for Strategic Affairs is Benjamin. J. Rhodes and a former Deputy Attorney General for Strategic Communications is Stephen Boyd. This, then, is, in brief, the skeletal structure of the US Department of Justice, a Department which has around 1,10,000 employees. The Deputy Attorney General is the COO of the organization, assisting the Attorney General in carrying out his duties. The Solicitor General is the fourth senior most official in the US Department of Justice and has a salary as per Executive Schedule Level 1.

US Ambassador to the UN

The US Ambassador to the UN under Trump was Kelly Knight Kraft, a former US Ambassador to Canada as noted earlier. She was preceded by Nikki Haley, an Indian American who traces her origins to Punjab. Before she was tipped for the Ambassador position to the UN, Nikki Haley, a typical ABCD (America Born Confused Desi) with a shaky hold over Punjabi, was a two-time Governor of South Carolina. While she backed President Trump in the 2020 standoff between him and Joe Biden, Haley expressed a desire to be future American Presidential candidate. The first US Ambassador to the UN was Edward Reilly Stettinius. Notable US Ambassadors to the UN include the suave former US President George Herbert Walker Bush Sr., a product of the Ivy League Yale, which incidentally is America's 3rd oldest University, former Secretary of State Madeliene Albright (under Clinton), former Illinois Governor, the legendary Adlai Ewing Stevenson who was noted for his demeanor and others.

The American Electoral System-Room for Conflicts Galore

America is a indestructible union of indestructible states [unlike India, which is a indestructible union of destructible states for e.g. it would not have been possible to do a Andhra, Jharkhand, Chattisgarh or Uttarakhand(until 2000 Uttaranchal) in the United States] where the states are sovereign entities within the American federal system with their own armed forces, Secretary of State, legal hierarchy, set of laws, and so on, all subsumed to the overall meaning of the American federal system. The American superstructure is sacrocant. All this means that each state has its own Election Commission with no centralized Election Commission like in India with the attendant coloring of the state's Election Commission policies with the ideological hues of ruling party of the state. Come election time, like now (2020) and there are conflicts galore with the result that the winner of the popular vote may still not become President as there is still the Electoral College vote to win (*a la* Hillary Clinton). The 2020 electoral mess was because of this anomaly in the American electoral system. The Indian Westminister model of parliamentary democracy is better and superior. America can ill afford to have this anomaly in what is otherwise a highly organized scheme of things which is difficult to beat and emulate. It reflects badly on its international image and may even be prone to foreign manipulation. It is worth remembering that foreign manipulation of elections is something all countries have to live with and America itself has done it. In fact, it has been the standard American practice for years and foreign countries esp. enemy ones may try to get back at America. Something like this was evident in the 2016 American election with allegations of Russian meddling in the elections.

American Presidents-Those at the Helm of the American Power Pyramid

Listing out the American Presidents, while George Washington is universally presumed to be the first American President, this is technically not true. For instance, the United States became independent in 1776, but it was not until 1780 that Washington took oath of office. So, who ruled the United States in the intervening period, a full four years, a relatively long period for a country to be headless? Are we to believe the United States was headless at the time? No. It was a man named John Hanson who ruled the United States during the time. "John who" you might say. But this is indeed true. It was John Hanson who ruled the United States in the intervening period. This is the real truth. However, effectively, George Washington (whose prior office was Commander-in-Chief of the Continental Army, as the U.S. Army was then known) is regarded as the first President of the United States. In Washington's time there were no political parties as it was felt at the time, perhaps with some justification, they posed a threat to the political quality of the polity, George Washington being the only American President not to be aligned to any political party, the second President was John Adams(the first American Vice-President ,the first American Secretary of State and the first American Ambassador to the Court of St. James, United Kingdom who brought remarkable talent to the job with a deep insight into foreign affairs) whose wife Abigail Adams was a bedtime story teller for children, Thomas Jefferson was the third American President(2nd American Vice President and a former US Ambassador to France he drafted the Declaration of Independence and is counted among the Founding Fathers of the United States), 4th American President James Madison(the 3rd American Vice President after whom Madison Avenue in New York is named and who played a pivotal role in the ratification of the American Constitution by signing the Federalist Papers along with Alexander Hamilton and John Jay, first Chief Justice of the US Supreme Court and as such is called the Father of the American Constitution), 5th American President James Monroe(a former US Ambassador to France and US Ambassador to the Court of St. James, United Kingdom) [the first five American Presidents along with

Benjamin Franklin (first American Ambassador to France who was also Louisiana and Pennsylvania Governor) are regarded as the founding fathers of America], John Quincy Adams, 6th American President and son of 2nd American President John Adams(whose offices held included Vice President, Secretary of State, US Ambassador to the Court of St. James United Kingdom. After the failure of the Francis Dana(that way the first US Ambassador to the Russian Empire) mission Adams was appointed as the first recognized US Ambassador to Russia, whose wife Louisa Adams became the first foreign born(she was a Briton born in London, and not counting those before the country existed) First Lady of the United States with Melania Trump(she was born in Sevro Meca, Slovenia on April 26th, 1970 and is 50) becoming the second, originally a Democrat, John Quicy Adams later switched loyalties to the Democratic Republican Party and in the 1830s swung over to the Whigs) Andrew Jackson,7th American President who was the first to use the word "Factory System", 8th American President Martin Van Buren(a former Secretary of State and a former US Ambassador to the Court of St. James, United Kingdom), 9th American President William Henry Harrison(a former Secretary of State who was the only American President to die in office when he died of pneumonia just 34 days into his term), 10th American President John Tyler(who was a former Secretary of State before assuming office as President), 11th American President James Knox Polk James.K.Polk(whose prior office was 13th Tennessee Governor and later 9th Speaker of the US House of Representatives and who died of cholera, at the time, a dreaded disease. A protege of Andrew Jackson, and a member of the Democratic Party he was an advocate of Jacksonian policies. The Vice President under him was George.M.Dallas), 12 American President Zachary Taylor(a US Army Colonel who became a national hero because of his victories in the Mexican-American Civil War), 13 American President Millard Fillmore, 14th American President Franklin. D. Pierce(whose prior office was US Minister to the Court of St. James, United Kingdom and who was a firm believer that the abolitionist movement was a fundamental threat to the unity of the nation), 15th American President James Buchanan(the only bachelor President of the United States whose prior office was US Ambassador to the Court of St. James, United Kingdom and before that US Ambassador to the Russian Empire), 16th American President the splendid Abraham Lincoln who is regarded as America's greatest ever President(a member of the GOP, his prior office was Congressman from Illinois's 7th Congressional District from 1847-1849), 17th American President Andrew Johnson who along with Trump is the only American President to be impeached in the U.S. House of Representatives, 18th American President Ulysses . S. Grant, 19th American President Rutherford B. Hayes, 20th American President James .A .Garfield who was assassinated, 21th American President Chester . A. Arthur, 22nd American President Grover Cleveland (Governor of New York and only American President to serve two non-consecutive terms), 23rd American President Benjamin Harrison(grandson of 9th American President William Henry Harrison creating the only grandfather-grandson presidential duo in US history), 24th American President Grover Cleveland(22nd American President), 25th American President William McKinley who was assassinated, 26th American President Theodore Roosevelt(25th American Vice- President and Nobel Peace Laureate. Contrary to popular perception, John F. Kennedy is not the youngest American President, Theodore Roosevelt is, all of 42 years 233 days as on the day he entered office.), 27th American President William Howard Taft (a former US Senator from Ohio whose prior office was Chief Justice of the US Supreme Court), 28th American President Woodrow Wilson(a Nobel Peace Laureate), 29th American President Warren .G. Harding, 30th American President Calvin Coolidge, 31st American President Herbert Hoover(a former Secretary of Commerce after whom the Hoover Dam in the United States is named, he died in the upscale Waldorf Astoria Hotel in New York of a heart attack), 32nd American President Harry .S. Truman(whose famous quote "The Navy forms the bulwark of our defense force as 3/4ths of the world is covered by water" made the United States primarily a naval power and a super power, 33rd U.S.

President the handsome Franklin Delano Roosevelt who signature fireside chats during World War 2 made him a lovable and affable figure all over the United States and who was the only American President to serve four consecutive terms after which the rules were changed to prevent such an eventuality from happening again, 34 U.S. President Dwight . D. Eisenhower (Ike as he was popularly known), 35th American President the charismatic John .F. Kennedy of the Kennedy clan with their tragic grandeur[who was the First Roman Catholic President of the United States [and who famously announced at Rice University that America would place a man on the moon which finds resonance in 2020 when NASA has announced the Artemis(sister of Apollo and Greek Goddess of Moon) program to place the first woman and the next man on the moon by 2024 and establish a sustainable human lunar presence on the moon by the end of the decade] whose prior office was Massachusetts Senator a post also occupied by his brother Edward Kennedy, another brother Robert. F Kennedy was Secretary of Justice and U.S. Attorney General as noted earlier. The eldest brother, Joseph Kennedy Jr died a premature death as a bomber pilot during World War 2 while the father, Joseph Kennedy Sr was US Ambassador to UK], 36th American President Lyndon .B.Johnson(US Vice President under President Kennedy), Richard Nixon[he along with his Vice President Spiro Theodore Agnew{who was the first Greek-American Governor of an American State(Maryland, other Maryland Governors include Millard .J. Tawes and Marvin Mandel) was impeached and both had to resign in the infamous Watergate scandal. Spiro Agnew became only the second American Vice President to resign, the other being James. C. Calhoun in 1832. Unlike Calhoun, Spiro Agnew had to resign the position as a result of a scandal.]

Richard Nixon, as is well known, was one among only three American Presidents [the other two being Bill Clinton and Donald Trump[whose impeachment was politically motivated, both the initial House conviction(as Democrats are in a majority there) and the subsequent Senate acquittal(as Republicans are in a majority here)]] to be impeached, Gerald Ford(an oil tycoon who owned Shell and under whom the Vice President was Hubert Humphrey), Jimmy Carter(a former Georgia Governor and peanut farmer who the Iranians had on the mat during the Islamic Revolution of the late 1970s), Ronald Reagan(former California Governor and B grade film actor who hit back at Hollywood for giving him the short shrift by becoming President), the Yale educated suave George Herbert Walker Bush Sr(a former US Ambassador to the United Nations who hit the campaign trail with the splash of tea mismatch and who appealed even to his Democrat opponent Bill Clinton on the campaign trail), the charismatic Bill Clinton(a former Arkansas Governor and outstanding intellectual who had the press eating out of his hands and great friend of India but who offered homilies to India on his pet CTBT), George Walker Bush Jr.(a former Texas Governor and Bush Sr.'s son known for his gaffes and about whom it was said Clinton's deputy Al Gore would have made a better President than him), the first Afro-American and first Muslim President Barack Hussein Obama(a native of Hawaii and known as black Kennedy who was New York Senator and whose 2020 book on India, A Promised Land, was a runaway bestseller), Donald Trump(only American President apart from 17th American President Andrew Johnson to be impeached in the US House of Representatives, Trump was born to Fred Trump and Mary Ann Macleod Trump(whose father was a fisherman, crofter and compulsory teacher in Mary's school) at Jamaica City Centre Medical Hospital in Queens, a borough of New York on 14th June, 1946 (age 74 years), went to Kew Forest School from 1959-1964, New York Military Academy from 1964-66, Fordham University from 1966-68 and picked up a B.A. Degree in Economics from the Wharton School of Economics of the University of Pennsylvania between 1969 to 1974 and is a real estate tycoon whose net worth(as per 2020 figures provided by Forbes magazine) stands at a whopping $ 250Cr. A political theorist and a political economist and TV personality who owns the Miss World and Miss Universe beauty pageants, Trump is a Republican now but his other political affiliations include the Democratic Party(up to 1989 and again from 2001-2009), America's Reform Party (from 1999 to 2001) and Independent(between 2011-2012). First Lady Melania Trump who speaks Serbian, German, French besides English and can manage a smattering of Italian as well, is only the second foreign born First Lady (she was born in Sevro Meca, Slovenia)(not including those before the country existed) of the United States after Louisa Adams, wife of 6th American President John Quincy Adams, who was born a Briton in London. The US Vice President under Trump was Mike Pence, a former Indiana Governor and Lt. Governor. Other American Vice Presidents include Nelson Rock feller under President Gerald Ford, Dick Cheney and others.

The Joe Biden Era- A New Dawn?

The new American President, Joseph Robinette 'Joe' Biden, a former Michigan Senator and Governor promises to unfold a new dawn. Joe Biden was born on November 20th 1942(age 78 years) in the rust-belt town of Scranton, Pennsylvania. Early on in life, he was brought close to America's systemic inequalities which sharpened his nose for politics and honed his skills as a liberal politician. His father, a car salesman, when faced with the economic doldrums, moved the family to Delaware where he grew up. In his younger days, Joe suffered from a stutter so bad that he was promptly dubbed 'Dash' by his friends and acquaintances. However, not only did he overcome the stutter, he helped others with stutter. Still, remnants of his stutter days marred his campaign trail when he called Massachusetts Governor Charles Duane 'Charlie' Baker, Charlie 'Parker.' He flaunts his blue collar credentials and takes pride from the fact that he is not part of the Ivy League Group of Schools having attended Arch Mere Academy, University of Delaware and The University of Pennsylvania. He suffered two tragedies. The first whammy hit him when his wife of 6 years (1966-72) Neillia Hunter who along with their infant daughter Naomi Campbell Biden died in a car crash in 1972. He met his present wife Jill Jacobs Biden in

1974 and the couple after going steady for a couple of years, married in 1977. Jill was a community teacher in Virginia Community Teaching Centre and says she has two passions- teaching and athletics esp. running marathons. In fact, as America's former SecondLady, she was taking teaching sessions abroad Air Force 2 and now she is likely to do the same abroad Air Force 1. The couple have two sons from Joe's first wife Neillia, Robert Hunter and Beau, and a daughter, Ashley from Joe's second marriage with Jill. Beau served as Delaware Attorney General before dying a premature death in 2015 due to brain cancer which is when the second tragedy surfaced in Joe's life. The older son, Hunter, a rather lacklustre figure, who faced problems of drug and alcohol abuse in his life, was discharged from the US Navy Reserve after testing positive for cocaine. However, he did serve a stint as CEO of Ukrainian gas company BAROSA which was when Trump piled charges of corruption at his door. While admitting to possible error of judgement, he denied any wrongdoing.

On the 2016 campaign trail which saw Trump become President, other Presidential hopefuls included Ohio Governor John Kasich, New Jersey Governor Chris Christie, Florida Senator Marco Rubio, Senator Ted Cruz, Texas Governor and George Walker Bush Jr.'s half brother Jeb Bush, former Hewlett Packard CEO Carly Fiorina and African- American neuro surgeon Ben Carson who led color to the campaign (Ben Carson was later absorbed into Donald Trump's cabinet as Secretary of Urban Development), Virginia Governor James Stewart 'Jim' Gilmore, New York Governor George Pataki, Maryland Governor Martin O' Malley, Kentucky Senator Rand Paul, Pennsylvania Senator Rick Santorum, Rhode Island Governor Lincoln Chaffee, Wisconsin Governor Jim Webb, Wisconsin Senator John Scott, former Texas Governor Rick Perry, Louisiana Governor Bobby Jindal, Harvard University Professor Lawrence Lessig all of the Republican Party, New York Senator Hillary Clinton (with her running mate former Virginia Governor Tim Kaine), Vermont Senator Bernard 'Bernie' Sanders both of the Democratic Party, Massachusetts Governor Gerald Johnson who with his running mate New Mexico Governor Bill Weld belongs to the Libertarian Party, and physician from Massachusetts Jill Stein who with her running mate Ajamu Baraka belongs to America's Green Party. Other candidates who scored prominently on the ballot included candidates of the Constitution Party and the Reform Party.

In the 2020 Presidential Election which saw Michigan Senator and former Michigan Governor Joe Biden of the Democratic Party become President along with his running mate California Senator and former California Attorney General Kamala Devi Shyamala Gopalan Harris whose mother is from Tamil Nadu in India and whose father, a Harvard University Professor from Jamaica, becoming Vice President, other Presidential candidates included senior American Senator from Massachusetts Elizabeth Ann Warren, Vermont Senator Bernard 'Bernie' Sanders (whose unravelling the election was witness to), Missouri Senator Amy Marie Klobuchar who is a member of the Missouri Farmers Party, the Missouri affiliate of the Democratic Party, junior American Senator from New Jersey Roy Booker, New York Mayor Bill de Blasio who the Democrats thought was the perfect spoil to President Trump's plans, Virgin Supreme and his running mate Jo Jorgenese of the Libertarian Party, Pete Butigieg, now Secretary of Transportation in President Biden's Cabinet, and of course Donald Trump and former Vice President Michael Mike Pence apart many, many others. Incidentally, Trump is only the first American President since Carter to serve only one term while Joe Biden is among 1 in 3 American Vice Presidents to become President.

The Second-in-Command -The Secretary of State

Secretaries of State include Gen. Alexander Haig (a former Supreme Allied Commander Europe (SACEAUR) with headquarters at Mons, Belgium reporting to the NATO Secretary General via the North Atlantic Military Committee during the Reagan Era), Gen. Colin. L. Powell (an Afro-American who is former Chairman, Joint Chiefs of Staff Committee), Condoleezza Rice (first Afro-American woman to become Secretary of State), Edward Reilly Stettinius (under Presidents Franklin Delano Roosevelt and Harry .S. Truman who was America's first UN Ambassador(between1945-46) apart from those already mentioned and numerous others.

Governors in the States

The Governors in the states include Ralph Northam, Governor of Virginia (a former Lt. Governor of Virginia), Lt. Governor Justin Edward 'Ed' Fairfax, a former US Attorney from Virginia, Attorney General Mark Rankin Herring, Governor of New Jersey Philip 'Phil' Murphy (a former Governor is Chris Christie who was a contender in the 2016 Presidential campaign which saw Donald Trump become President), Lt. Governor Sheila Oliver (the first Afro-American Governor of an American State), Attorney General Gurbir. S .Grewal (first Sikh Attorney General of an American State), Florida Governor Ronald 'Ron' Dion DeSantis, Lt. Governor Carlos Lopez Cantera (first Hispanic Lt. Governor of an American State), (the first Governor of Florida was William Dunn Moseley who was born in North Carolina and died at Boca Raton, Florida, the first Governor before the drawing up of the American Constitution being William Washington Jones Kelly, William W. J. Kelly and the first Lt. Governor after the drawing up of the American Constitution being Milton Harvey Malbry, Milton. H. Malbry ,Texas Governor Gregory Wayne Abbott, Greg Abbott, who was the state's 48th Attorney General(the first Texas Governor was James Pinkney Henderson), Texas Lt. Governor is Daniel Scott Goeb Patrick Danny Scott Goeb Patrick, a realty television star and TV host ,West Virginia Governor James Conley Justice II, a coal mining baron and agricultural businessman who with a net worth of $1.9 billion is the richest man in West Virginia and one of the richest men in the United States and is married to Cathy Justice, Utah Governor Spencer Cox who was recently elected and is a former Lt. Governor of the State, North Carolina Governor Roy Ashberry Cooper III, a Democrat and an attorney who went to North Carolina University at Chapel Hill where he did his BA and JD, California Governor Gavin Newsom, Massachusetts Governor Charles Duane 'Charlie' Baker who went to Kellogg Management School, Michigan Governor Gretchen Esther Whitmer, Mississippi Governor Tate Reeves, a Republican, Missouri Governor Mike Parson, Missouri Lt. Governor Mike Kehoe, Pennsylvania Governor Thomas 'Tom' Wolf the first Jewish Governor of Pennsylvania being Milton Jerrold Shapp who was the State's 40th governor and served from 1971-79, Louisiana Governor John Bel Edwards, the Georgia Governor Brian Porter Kemp, Wisconsin Governor Anthony Steven Evers, Ohio Governor Michael 'Mike' D Wine, Maryland Governor Lawrence H Larry Hogan, Alabama Governor Kay Ellen Ivey, Arizona Governor Douglas Anthony 'Doug' Ducey who incidentally was Cold Stone Creamy CEO before he jumped into politics(Arizona, incidentally, is one of 7 American States where there is no post of Lt. Governor), New York Governor Andrew Mario Cuomo whose father Mario Cuomo was also a three time Governor of New York, Illinois Governor J.B. Pritzker of the Pritzker Group of Industries, Tennessee Governor William 'Bill' Lee, the 3rd longest serving Governor in American history, former South Dakota Governor William John Janklow who was born on 13th September 1939 in Illinois, Chicago and died in Sioux Falls, South Dakota on 12th February and belonged to the United States Marine Corps other South Dakota Governors being Richard Kneip and Harvey Wollen, former North Dakota Governor Jack Stewart Dalrymple, Kansas Governor John Anderson, Arkansas Governor William Asa 'Bill' Hutchinson II, Rhode Island Governor is Dan McKee as noted earlier, Alaska Governor Mike Dunleavy, Hawaii Governor David Ige, Montana Governor Greg Gianforte, Montana Lt. Governor Kirstjan Juras, Indiana Governor Eric Holcomb, Indiana Lt. Governor Suzanne Ann Crouch, New Hampshire Governor Christopher 'Chris' Sununu, North Dakota current Governor Douglous 'Doug' Burgum, North Dakota Lt. Governor Brent.R Sanford, Delaware Governor John Charles Carney, Vermont Governor Phillip 'Phil' Scott, Vermont Lt. Governor David Zuckerman and 30th Governor of New Mexico William Blaine

Harrison III who was Governor from 2003-2011 are but some of the vast galaxy of American Governors and Lt. Governors ever.

The Senators

American Senators include senior American Senator from Massachusetts Elizabeth Ann Warren who incidentally made a broadside against India on Kashmir, junior American Senator from New Jersey Roy Booker, Missouri Senator Amy Marie Klobuchar, former senior American Senator from Utah Orin Hatch who incidentally is the longest serving American Senator ever and who recently stood down, former junior American Senator from Utah Mike Lee, Massachusetts Senator and former Massachusetts Governor Mitt Romney, a Republican, former Massachusetts Senator the world famous former US President John .F. Kennedy and his brother Edward Kennedy who was also a Massachusetts Senator, at 88(born 1933), the oldest sitting American Senator Dianne Feinstein of California who is a former Mayor of San Francisco, the oldest lived American Senator in history Cornelius Cole who died at 102, the longest serving American Senator ever Robert. C. Byrd who served from 1959-2010, who is followed by Daniel .K. Inouye who is followed by Storm Thurmond, former American President William Howard Taft who was Ohio Senator, Michigan Senator Joe Biden who holds the record for being the youngest Senator ever, Senator Brien Mc Mohan who was instrumental in the decision not to appoint Dr .Robert .J. Oppenheimer to the General Advisory Committee of the now defunct U. S Atomic Energy Commission. The mid-term elections to the U. S. Senate (2019) threw up Senators Joe Manchin III of West Virginia, Senator Beto O' Rourke and Josh Hawley who defeated Claire Mc Caskill, former Virginia Senator Jennifer Wexton who won an election to the U. S. Congress defeating former U. S. Congresswoman Barbara Comstock, six time Arizona Senator, Vietnam war hero(whose long-range bomber was downed in Vietnam) and former Presidential candidate John Mc Cain, six time

Arizona Senator the powerful Jeff Flake, and Idaho Senator Chuck Grassley are some of the American Senators. State Senators include Michigan State Senator Margaret O' Brien, Ohio State Senator Sean O' Brien and New York State Senator Ted O' Brien, and North Carolina State Senator Mujtaba. A. Mohammed.

The Congressmen

Abigail Ann Spanberger, a C. I. A Operative and a Democrat, who defeated her Republican opponent Dan Brat, a Republican Caucus and Tea Party member(a conservative movement) in the mid-term election of 2019 and became Congresswoman for Virginia's 7th Congressional District whose district includes most of the northern suburbs of Richmond and some exurban areas of neighboring Fredericksburg and who won re-election to the U.S. House from the same district in Election 2020, the first Muslim Congresswoman Rashida Tlaib and Ilhan Omar, both Palestinian Americans, New York Congressman Steve King, Indian American Congressmen and Congresswoman include the popular Pramila Jayapal from Washington's 13th Congressional District, Ro Khanna from California's 17th Congressional District that includes Silicon Valley, Raja Krishnamoorthy from Texas, Dr.Ami Bera from California's 7th Congressional District and Suraj Patel from New York all of whom won re-election in the elections of 2020. Prominent among the losers are Sarah Rao from Colorado, Anita Malik and others. Many of them along with Surgeon General during the Obama Administration Vivek Murthy and 8 women are understood to be among the people who are likely to find a place in the Joe Biden Cabinet. They have since been accomodated in the Cabinet..Virginia Congressmen and women include former Senator Jennifer Wexton, former Virginia Congresswoman Barbara Comstock, and Alexandra Ocasio Cortez. The oldest black Congressman is John .C.Conyers from Michigan's 13th Congressional District and then there was, of course, India's good friend in the U.S. Congress Stephen Solarz whom Gen. Zia ul Haq of Pakistan called India's paid agent in the

U.S. Congress.

America-Taliban Agreement

The head of the U.S. and NATO Forces in Afghanistan is Gen Scott Miller who is preceded by Gen. John Nicholson. The first Commander is Stanley Allen McCrystal, Stanley. A. McCrystal (a graduate of U.S. Army War College and U.S. Infantry School who was appointed in 2009 and since 2010 the Afghan Mission Network has served as an information sharing platform for U.S. and NATO troops in Afghanistan. America and NATO, however, have started a phased withdrawal from Afghanistan consequent on the Taliban sticking to its part of the agreement under an agreement struck between the two. As per the terms of the agreement, America and NATO will withdraw troops in two phases. In the first phase, America will withdraw 14,000 troops and in the second 8,000 eventually completing a complete withdrawal. All this is, of course, contingent on the Taliban sticking to its part of the agreement under the terms of which it will abjure violence, respect the rights of Afghan men and women and will fall within the ambit of the Afghan Constitution. All the key players in the Afghan cauldron-America, Russia, China, Iran and Pakistan besides the Taliban will ensure that this happens. However, as a senior American administration official himself admitted the road to an elusive peace is long, tenuous and arduous and full of thorns and the agreement may collapse any time into a bottomless vortex of violence. Needless to say, any fragmentation of Afghanistan will have a centrifugal impact on the unity of Pakistan. The Afghan government of President Mohammed Ashraf Ghani has since fallen and the Taliban have taken over the country and Afghanistan is in a state of flux with no government in place. The Taliban have sacked the last remaining Minister of the previous government Waheed Majroh.

Directors of Strategic Communications

American Directors of Strategic Communications include the incumbent, Kate Bedingfield, Bill Shine, Hope Hicks, the mouthy financier Mercedes Schlapp, Anthony Scaramucci, Sean Spicer, Omarosa Manigault (a reality T.V. Star and an alumni of University of Florida who studied at the United Theological Seminary), Acting Director Sean Spicer, Jen Psaki, Pat Buchanan, Margita White, George Stephanopoulos, Margaret Tutwiler, Acting Director Anita Dunn, Karen Hughes, Ann Lewis, Kevin Sullivan, Jerry Warren, Ken Clawford and the very first Director Herbert .G. Klein, Herb G. Klein and others.

However, American officials have shown a high rate of attrition under Trump on account of the former President's whimsical ways. In the words of former White House Deputy Chief of Staff Katie Walsh "Trying to determine what the President wants is like trying to determine what a baby wants"

U.S. Trade Representative

A former U.S. Trade Representative is Ambassador Carla Hills and the American Trade Representative under Trump, Ambassador Robert Lighthizer executed the NAFTA Deal in consonance with then Japanese Minister of Industry, Trade and Economy Hiroshige Seko and the then Mexican Secretary of the Economy Ildefonso Guajardo Villareal, an economist and politician belonging to the Institutional Revolutionary Party of former Mexican President Enrique Pena Nieto, a development then Mexican Foreign Minister Luis Videgaray Caso called "good for Mexico, good for North America." The incumbent is Katherine Tai, as noted earlier.

The United Kingdom

The Prime Minister- the Epicentre of Power

Coming to the United Kingdom, the British Prime Minister is, of course, Alexander Pfeffel de Boris Johnson who was born in the United States and who has been Prime Minister of Britain and leader of the Conservative Party since 2019, Foreign Secretary of the United Kingdom from 2016 to 2018 and before that London Mayor from 2008 to 2016 and Uxbridge MP from 2001 to 2008 and since 2008 has been Henley MP. The first British Prime Minister was William Petty, 2nd Earl of Shelburne, 1st Marquess of Lansdowne who was also the first British Home Secretary. However, in modern times the first British Prime Minister was Robert Anthony Eden who was Prime Minister from 1956-1959 and Foreign Secretary from 1951-1955. Other British Prime Ministers include William Pitt (1st Earl of Liverpool who at 24yrs is the youngest world leader ever and lived in the 19th century), Robert Walpole, 1st Earl of Oxford, Harold Macmillan in the 1960s, James Callaghan, Winston Churchill, Clement Attlee both of whom were also Defence Secretaries apart from which Churchill also held the Home portfolio. Some other names which come to mind are the incumbent's predecessor Theresa May of the Tories who was also Home Secretary and Maidenhead MP, David Cameron, Gordon Brown, the wimp Neville Chamberlain who like Jimmy Carter in the United States was more moral than many British Prime Ministers but whose moral stature collapsed on the ground of the realities of geopolitics underscoring the eternal truism that in politics and esp. international politics aspects like national interest count more than morals and principles although the importance of the latter in politics and international political life cannot be denied. Of course, hundreds of other British Prime Ministers dot the political canvass of the United Kingdom and who made the United Kingdom the great power that it is today.

The Home Secretary

A member of the Cabinet, the Privy Council and the National Security Council, Her Majesty's Secretary of State for the Home Office or Secretary of State for Home or simply the Home Secretary is one of the four great offices of state. The office has been occupied by many luminaries and others like the very first Home Secretary William Petty, 2nd Earl of Shelburne, 1st Marquess of Lansdowne who was also the first British Prime Minister as noted earlier. He was followed by Lord Fredrick North, Lord North(MP for Banbury) Other British Home Secretaries include Charles Phillipe Yorke, Herbert Gladstone, MP for Leeds West, Herbert Samuel, MP for Dorchester and later in his second term MP for Morpeth, James Graham (MP for Devonport), George Gray (MP for Dorchester, Northumberland), John Russell (MP for Stroud), Robert Lowe, Richard Ryder, Robert Peel (MP for Tiverton), Sir Robert Peel FRS (MP for three constituencies), R.A.Cross, Hugh Childers, Henry Mathews, Reginald McKenna, Reginald Maudling (MP for Barnet), Herbert Stanley Morrison, Henry Austin Bruce, Kenneth Baker, James Callaghan (later a Prime Minister of UK), the charismatic 'Bull Dog' PM Winston Churchill (Dundee MP) who also held the Defence portfolio having succeeded Emmanuel 'Manny' Shinwell in the job, Kenneth Clarke, Alan Johnson, Michael Howard, Henry Petty Fitzmaurice 3rd Marquess of Lansdowne KG PC FRS, a British statesman who was known as Henry Petty between 1784 to 1809 and who in a ministerial career spanning nearly half a century served in a variety of roles including as Home Secretary, Lord Chancellor of the Exchequer and Lord President of the Council, Douglas Hurd, Leon Brittan, David Blunkett, John Reid, John Simon, Jack Straw, Roy Jenkins, William Sturgeous Browne, Spencer Horatio Walpole, John Anderson, Arthur Henderson, Robert Carr (MP for Carshalton now split into Carshalton and Wellington), Jacqui Smith, Marilyn Rees, H. H. Asquith, Charles Ritchie, Charles Clarke, Theresa May(one of the only four British Home Secretaries to become PM and Maidenhead MP), Amber Rudd (MP for Hastings and Rye), Sajid Javid (a Pakistani origin British Citizen, Bromsgrove MP and later Lord Chancellor of the Exchequer) and finally the incumbent Home

Secretary Priti Sushi Patel, an Indian-origin Gujarati British citizen who earlier served as International Development and Equal Opportunities Secretary(and Employment Secretary) whom former British Prime Minister David Cameron described as a possible "future British Prime Minister". The Empire striking back?

The British Monarchy

Coming to the British monarchy, the present British Queen, Elizabeth II, the grand -daughter of Queen Victoria of Victorian Era fame, ascended the throne on February 6th, 1952 upon the death of her father King George IV. The King is, of course, King Phillip and their son Prince Charles is married to Camilla Parker Bowles, Duchess of Cornwall and they both are together known as Duke and Duchess of Cornwall. Unlike his deceased first wife Princess Diana Spencer, Camilla Parker Bowles will not become the future Queen of England. Instead, Prince Charles and Lady Diana Spencer's older son Prince Williams and his wife Kate Williams daughter will. The future England Queen's school going brother Prince George recently faced a spate of terror threats. Their younger son is Prince Harry who is wedded to former Hollywood star Meghan Marple whose son is Prince Archie. Prince Harry and Princess Meghan Marple are known as the Duke and Duchess of Cambridge. The first King of England, King Egbert (8th Century ACE), who upon his return from the Court of Charlemagne ruled all of Anglo-Saxon England from Wessex outwards earning the title Bretwalda. The first King of the world was King Charles Athelstan, earlier called King Charles I. Among latter day monarchs of Britain were the Anglo-Normans of the 8^{tH}-9th Century ACE. The first Queen of England, Elizabeth I (who, incidentally, was the Queen of England when the British government took over the administration of India from the English East India Company), a contemporary of the 15th Century ACE, was the last of the House of Tudors.

The Three Provinces of England

The three provinces of England, Scotland, Northern Ireland and Wales, each headed by a First Minister who is responsible to the Cabinet of the province, relations with the rest of the United Kingdom, with Europe and the wider world(in Scotland's case) and in Scotland and Northern Ireland's case coordinate the meetings of the Cabinet under the devolved government of these three provinces of England. In Northern Ireland's case there is a Deputy First Minister as well. While the Deputy First Minister's position is in no way inferior to that of the First Minister, the First Minister is first among equals.

Scotland

The very first Scottish First Minister was Donald Dewar, Glasgow Southside MP, followed by Acting First Minister Jim Wallace MP for Orkney Islands, followed by Henry McLeish, Central Fife MP, who in turn was followed by John McConnell, Motherwell and Wishaw MP, to be followed by Scottish National Party's leader and Aberdeenshire MP(since 2011) Alex Salmond who on 7th November 2012 surpassed the earlier record held by John McConnell as the longest serving Scottish First Minister and who had to resign after his Independence Referendum failed to muster the required majority paving the way for the present First Minister of Scotland Nicola Sturgeon, Glasgow Govan MP and Scottish National Party leader who too twice failed to push through a key Independence Referendum ahead of Brexit, but, unlike Alex Salmond, did not have to resign.

Northern Ireland

The First First Minister of Northern Ireland was Seamus Mallon while the first Deputy First Minister was David Trimble another Acting First Minister being Jim Wallace while another Deputy First Minister was John Swinton. A third First Minister was Alun Michael AM while under him Deputy First Minister was Mike German. From 2001-2009 First Minister of Northern Ireland was Democratic Unionist Party leader Peter David Robertson who continued as

Democratic Unionist Party leader until 2015 when Arlene Foster took charge as Democratic Unionist Party leader and in 2016 Arlene Foster took over as the First Minister of Northern Ireland with Michelle O' Neill as incumbent Deputy First Minister. The new First Minister who took charge 2021 is John Givan while Michelle O' Neill continues to be the Deputy First Minister.

Direct Rule First Ministers

Direct Rule First Ministers include John Reid, John Givan and others.

With regard to Northern Ireland, it is worth noting that the British Government under Prime Minister Boris Johnson is going ahead with its plans to construct a wall all along the 500 km land border between Britain and its province of Northern Ireland under Article 501 of the of the English Constitution thereby ending the long-standing practice of porous borders with Northern Ireland something which has brought the Conservative government of Boris Johnson in conflict with the EU and the wider world ahead of Brexit which will start on midnight of January 31st 2021(The UK is now out of the EU) once Article 50 of the Lisbon Treaty which calls for the disentanglement of Britain from the European Union is set in motion with 2020 having been a transitory year in which Britain has been trying to negotiate a free trade and other agreements with the European Union, an enterprise in which it seems to have largely succeeded.

Wales

The First Minister of Wales is Mark Drakeford and his predecessor First Minister is Carwyn Jones who once said that India could serve as a gateway for trade with Europe.

Incidentally, a former Group Leader of West Minister, John Wilson some time back died at the age of 71. Further, the individual currencies of the Euro Zone, notable the German Deutsche Mark, Spanish Peso, French Franc, the Italian Lira as also the currencies of poor nations like Estonia and Slovakia have long since ceased to exist and they have subsumed themselves to the Euro. Such an approach is not feasible in individualistic England with the Pound

Sterling reigning supreme. The Leader of the Opposition in the House of Commons, the Shadow Prime Minister, is Labour's Jeremy Corbyn, a sworn pacifist and Socialist who opposed Britain's Iraq War and who has gone on record saying he would dismantle Britain's Trident nuclear submarines were he to come to power. Mr. Corbyn has also promised radical changes in Britain once he is in the saddle. The Leader of the Liberal Party is Tim Farrow.

First Lord of the Admiralty

British First Lord of the Admiralty include Albert Victor Alexander, A.V. Alexander, 1st Earl of Hillsborough who was thrice First Lord of the Admiralty including during the crucial phases of World War II and later Defense Secretary under Prime Minister Clement Atlee, who was preceded by Branden Bracken and succeeded by George Hall. Albert Victor Alexander was preceded as Defense Secretary by Emmanuel Manny Shinwell and succeeded by Winston Churchill. He was also Grand Duchy of Lancaster, a post in which he was preceded by Hugh Dalton and succeeded by The Viscount Swinton.

Lord Chancellor of the Exchequer

The first British Lord Chancellor of the Exchequer then called Lord High treasurer or Finance Minister in other countries with oversight over the Treasury was Eustace of Fauconberg, a medieval Bishop of London from 1221 to 1228. However, Hervey de Stanton was the first Chancellor of the Exchequer during the Kingdom of England period. More recent British Chancellors of the Exchequer include George Osborne who was followed by Phillip Hammond (a former British Foreign Secretary) who in turn was followed by the Pakistani origin Sajid Javid to be followed by the present Chancellor of the Exchequer Indian origin Rishi Sunak, a son-in-law of Infosys Supremo Narayan Murthy and a man being incresingly touted as a possible replacement to PM Johnson who is involved in a ugly, unseemly betting scandal. Alistair Darling was the Chancellor under Prime Minister Gordon Brown. The Chief Secretary to the Treasury is the Rt.Hon.Simon Clark MP who was preceded by Rishi Sunak. The Governor of the Bank of England is Mark Carney who was preceded by Mervyn Allister King, Baron King of Lothbury KG GBE DL FBA, a British economist and public servant who was later an MP.

The Defence Secretary

The first British Her Majesty's Principal Secretary of State for Defence or simply Defence Secretary was Peter Thorneycroft, a former British Chancellor of the Exchequer, the incumbent British Defence Secretary is the Rt. Hon. Ben Wallace, who was preceded by Penelope Mary Penny Mordaunt, a former British International Development Secretary (and Portsmouth North MP) and Women and Equal Opportunities Secretary who in that role paid a controversial secret visit to Israel where she met top level Israeli politicians, a move which cost her her job. However, she was later promoted as Defence Secretary after the heat had settled down. As Britain's Defence Secretary she went on record saying Britain does not need sixth generation fighter aircraft. She was preceded by Gavin Alexander Williamson, now Education Secretary who in turn was preceded by Sir Michael Cathel Fallon KCB who served as Defence Secretary from 2014-2017 and who as a member of the Conservative Party was MP for Sevenoaks from 1997 to 2019 and before that was Darlington MP from 1983 to 1992. However, he had to put in his papers after sex abuse charges were piled on him. The Minister of State for the Armed Forces was Col. John Mark Lancaster (Weisbridge MP) under former Prime Minister Theresa May.

The Foreign Secretary

The first British Foreign Secretary with oversight over the Foreign Offices and British missions abroad and the diplomatic corps in London was Charles James Fox who was followed by Foreign Secretaries George Manning, William Hague, David Milibind, Douglous Hurd, Jack Straw, Phillip Hammond (later Chancellor of the Exchequer), Prime Minister Boris Johnson, Jeremy Hunt (a former Health Secretary) and the Dominic Raab(a former Housing Secretary under former Conservative Prime Minister Theresa May) and the incumbent Elizabeth 'Liz' Truss and others.

The Minister of State for Foreign Affairs under Prime Minister May was Alistair Burt who at the time, in a bid to break the ice with Iran, paid a visit to Iran and met Iran's Supreme Leader Ayatollah Khamenei and broke butter with him.

Other senior British Ministers include former Fuel and Power Ministers, Emmanuel Manny Shinwell and Nicholas Cook and a host of others who held the same portfolio. A former British International Trade Secretary was Liam Fox.

The British Minister for Business, Enterprise and Industrial Strategy under May was Greg Clark. The Secretary of International Development in the May Government, Penelope Mary 'Penny' Mordaunt, MP for Portsmouth North, had to put in her papers after a controversial secret visit to Israel where she held parleys with high-level Israeli officials, something which opened up a pandora's box in Britain. Dominic Raab is also a former Brexit Secretary, a position in which he quit over Prime Minister Theresa May's Brexit Deal which now not only has the stamp of the British Parliament but Britain is out of the EU(a process which was set in motion by Article 50 of the Lisbon Treaty which calls for the disentanglement of Britain from the European Union), after a year-long transition period in 2020 in which Britain tried to wriggle out a free trade deal with the EU, an effort in which it seems to have succeeded. The highly individualistic British obviously seem to be enjoying the imaginary paradise (may we call it fool's paradise) they seem to have locked themselves up in. However, I am afraid, in this, they may have painted themselves into a corner as Britain has long ago become the small island it always was. However, before everybody jumps to conclusions, let me rush to assuage ruffled British feathers and remind the world that Britain still has a powerful military and there is the further fact that England is part of the Big-5 which after all is the thrust of this article. This is a reality we have to contend with although voices are being heard to include the emerging economies of the world like India, Japan, Germany and Brazil among the Big-5 as the stereotype of the Big-5 may no longer fit the facts as new power centers have emerged.

Coming to the junior ministers and MPs in the Theresa May administration, a former Housing Secretary and Deputy Brexit Secretary is Steve Banker. Labor Brexit Secretary during the time of May was Keir Starmer. Significantly, in India before the abrogation of Article 370 former Jammu and Kashmir Chief Minister Farooq Abdullah, before his arrest and subsequent release along with other Kashmiri leaders, while calling for a more tolerant policy on the part of the Indian Government, called for "porous borders" between India and Jammu and Kashmir of the kind that existed between Britain and its province of Northern Ireland before the wall was erected by the Boris Johnson Government. However, things have changed in both the UK and India and if the wall is a reality in the UK revocation of Article 370 is a reality in India.

Other ministers and MPs during the time of Theresa May are senior ministers, Works and Pensions Secretary Esther McVey and Permanent Under Secretary for Parliamentary Affairs Ann Marie Travelyan. Indian origin Sailesh Vara was Minister of State for Northern Ireland (he was prominent among the Ministers who quit over Brexit. a position also occupied at various times by Chloe Smith, John Penrose, Nicholas 'Nick' Hurd, James Reid, Baron Reid of Cardowan PC (Reid was also later Secretary of State for Northern Ireland and Secretary of State for Scotland apart from being, of course, Home Secretary and Defence Secretary), Julian Smith who was described by Irish President Michael D. Higgins as among Britain's finest, Hugo Swire, Andrew Robathan and others. The present Secretary of State for Northern Ireland is the Rt. Hon. Brandon Lewis. Coming back to the May Government, under May, there was one Pakistani-origin Minister, Rehman Chisti and one Sri Lankan-origin minister Ranil Jayawardene in what was a proportionate representation to the Indian sub-continent in the British cabinet. Both of these ministers quit over the direction Brexit negotiations were taking. The Transport Minister was Boris Johnson's brother, Jo Johnson. The Minister of Universities, Science, Research and Religion was Samuel Phillip 'Sam' Gymah who prevailed upon the Conservative Whip to pass a motion of censure against the Theresa May Government in the House of Commons. Incidentally, at the time, as many as 10 ministers expressed disapproval over Miss May's Brexit moves and called for a no-confidence motion against her government. Key among those who engineered this split was then Foreign Secretary and present Prime Minister Boris Johnson. The present Attorney General Sue Ellen Cassiana 'Suella' Braverman was then Fareham MP. She is also one prominent 'Indian' face in the British Cabinet. Other important officials in the Theresa May Government include Johnny Luther Mercer, East Lancashire MP Tracey Ann Crouch, Trade Secretary John McDowell, Conservative backbencher Anna Soubry, Labour MP Yasmin Quereshi, Labour MP and Shadow Chancellor of the Exchequer, Niel Kinnock, a sort of a Opposition Leader with no constitutional sanction and Gareth Stace, Head of the British Steel Body.

The Cabinet Secretary

The various Cabinet Secretaries include the incumbent Simon Case, his predecessor Sir Mark Sedwill, Jeremy Heywood, the inaugural holder Sir Maurice Hankey and others.

The Boris Johnson Government

Top ministers in the Johnson Government include present Secretary of Petroleum and Natural Gas and former International Development Secretary Alok Verma, Speaker of the 650-member House of Commons, Lindsay Hoyle who was preceded by John Bercow, Principal Deputy Speaker Eleanor Lang who is a former two-time Deputy Speaker, Secretary of State of Health Matt Hancock, Carshalton and Wellington MP Elliot Coulborn who in a giant-felling act felled long standing MP Thomas Anthony 'Tom' Brake, one time Home Secretary and Carshalton MP(at that time the constituency was known only as Carshalton, later Wellington was clubbed with Carshalton and the constituency came to be known as Carshalton and Wellington, European Parliament Constituency- South London, during the days before Brexit) Robert Carr and others. To pen a personal note, Prime Minister Johnson is a bachelor (although he has a girlfriend, Carrie Symonds which is in keeping with the current British reality in an age when the relentless onslaught of 'modernity' has snowballed into a crescendo and is chipping away at family values and age-old Britain seems to be no exception to this global reality in the global village that we live in today.).

Post-Brexit Reality

Post-Brexit Britain seems to in danger of losing its long-standing international pre-eminence and is in danger of being isolated in Europe (and the world) and the death knell may well have been sounded on Europe's second biggest economy, an economy which still punches much above its weight in international politics and economics, yet pulls no punches when it comes to preserving its individuality. In this connection, it is worthy of mention that with Brexit now a reality, Britain could well profit from its 'Special Relationship' with sole Superpower, America and emerging economy India. Otherwise, it could well be a case of the sun finally setting on the British 'Empire'.

The French Gendarme

The French Power Structure

Coming to French politics, at the apex of the French Power Pyramid is the current President of France, Emmanuel Macron touted as leader of the 'Free World' who at 40 is one of the youngest leaders in the world. He is a political independent. After the French Revolution which saw the codification of the Rights of Man into the French Constitution (into which the Indian Constitution digs heavily apart from drawing from the American Bill of Rights), France became a democracy and a Republic (as opposed to the UK which is a constitutional monarchy). Following the French example (and esp. after the Treaty of Versailles), many of the countries of the world starting with the United States upgraded their diplomatic representation from the lower Minister Plenipotentiary (who is a representative of a Government) to the higher Ambassadorial (who is a representative of a Sovereign) level. It was also the threshold, watershed period when the United States grew in population and economic strength till the later climax when there was a paradigm shift, a power switch in political power from the United Kingdom to the United States. The French Prime Minister is Edourd Charles Phillippe, a lawyer by profession. He is a former member of the Union for a Popular Movement, now known as the Republicans. The French Finance Minister is Bruno Le Maire, preceded by Michel Sapin who is preceded by former IMF Managing Director and current President of the European Central Bank, Christine Legarde. The French Interior Minister is Christophe Castener, preceded by Gerard Coullomb whose head rolled and he had to put in his papers after a spate of protests by yellow vests against President Macron's fuel tax. Mr. Coullomb is preceded by Bruno Le Roux and Bernard Cazeneuve,a former French Prime Minister. Other French Interior Ministers include former Prime Minister Manuel Volls former French President, Francois Mitterrand, former French President Nicholas Sarkozy, former French President and Prime Minister Alain Juppe, former French President Francois Hollande and others. The French Foreign Minister is Jean Yves Le Drien(who as Defense Minister was called France's salesman for his ability to sell niche defense technology to other countries including India which made several defense purchases during his tenure as Defense Minister). Before him, the Foreign Office was headed by Laurent Fabius. The French Minister of the Armed Forces or Defense Minister is Florence Parly(who was in India couple of years back to put across the Rafale and Scorpene deal which is now part of the Indian armory) and before that was the scandal tainted Sylvie Goulard who was sacked pending a magisterial enquiry in to alleged misuse of European parliamentary funds by her party, the French Socialist Party. Prior to her the Defense Minister was Jean Yves Le Drien. One further French Defense Minister is Michelle Alliot Marie during whose tenure India clinched the Scorpene submarine deal. In what could be a chink in the French armor in Africa, a French Barkhane

Defense Force (along with 9 other African nations) is fighting terrorists in Africa's Niger, apart from other countries and French troops have been deployed in war-torn Central African Republic and they have placed under the command of Gen. Franscisco Soriano. And, of course, as noted in an earlier article the French are fighting the Ansar Dine in the tinder box that is Mali, esp. Northern Mali, in a conflict that threatens to envelope neighboring countries in a region that is already volatile. Needless to say, French troops are playing a proactive and pivotal role in other flashpoints and trouble spots of the world as the French Gendarme still wields the baton and in the post-Brexit era and Madamosielle France can cherish hopes of upstaging the UK as a new power center of the world. However, all this has to be tempered with the fact that 21st Century will be an Asian century primarily powered by China in the immediate future and India in the long run [and, of course, there remains the fact of European integration (the EU was handed over the 2012 Nobel Peace Prize for making war unthinkable in Europe. Incidentally, in this connection former French Foreign Minister Robert Schuman(1951) in tandem with Jean Monnet, first and founder President of the European Coal and Steel Community, a touchstone and cornerstone of European Integration, made a invaluable contribution to European unity.)] and nobody can wish away Big Brother America. Interestingly, ASEAN is also emerging as a new trading bloc, even as the Russian bear gets increasingly assertive threatening to swallow even the mighty United States.

Those at the apex include French President Emmanuel Macron, his predecessor Francois Hollande(who sided with Rahul Gandhi and the Congress on the Rafale Deal prompting the Modi government to engage in some grandstanding and allege that there was an international plot taking place against Mr. Modi), Nicholas Sarkozy(with his 'wall flower' wife Carla Bruni and other 'wall flower' Ministers to use a phrase used by his former wife), the Socialist Francois Mitterrand who tried to dispose of the polluted aircraft carrier Clemenceau to India which was scrap fit for the Alang ship breaking yard, Valery Giscard De Estiang, Alain

Juppe(also a Prime Minister), the colossus Charles De Gaulle who led the French Resistance against Germany during World War II once famously remarking "With Germany as its neighbor, France has to sleep with one eye open, and with a nuclear Germany on its borders, it has to sleep with both eyes open" and many, many others. However, Herr Germany (and Japan) seem to have been tamed down, with them even voluntarily giving up their territorial ambitions and the German need for "lebensraum" so prevalent during World War-II under a despotic, criminal and autocratic leader(who the German people, to their shame, all 60 million of them, followed blindly having no two opinions about it) seems to be well and truly a thing of the past. French Prime Ministers include the incumbent Edourd Charles Phillippe, his predecessor, Bernard Cazeneuve, a former Interior Minister the Socialist Manuel Volls, Alain Juppe, Jean Pierre Ayrault and numerous others.

Prior to the 2016 Election which saw Emmanuel Macron win the mandate, the principal contenders for President included the right-wing Francois Fillon who won a conservative primary before his political career was nixed on the altar of a snowballing expenses scandal involving his British born wife Penelope Cruz and children, former Prime Minister Manuel Volls who was the Socialist pick for President but stood little chance of getting elected, former Economy Minister Arnaud Monteabourg, far-right leader Marine Le Pen(who once came within a whisker of becoming President, shocking Europe and the world), Mr. Macron himself(Mr. Macron was, in fact one of the dark horses) and others. Justice Minister within the French Cabinet is Nicole Belleubet.

French Posts and Telecommunications Ministers, a ministry which has been known by different names in different times, include Frances Sagard who in consonance with then French Ambassador to India Andre Goss inaugurated the Alliance Francaise in Bangalore in the presence of then Chief Minister of Karnataka R. Gundu Rao. Others French Posts and Telecommunications Ministers(earlier known by its earlier avatar, as Ministry of Posts and Telegraphs and other names), include John

Walsh and a host of others.

Vichy France as France was referred to under Phillipe Petain which included parts of the Unoccupied Free Zone(during the time of Nazi Germany) as far south as Algeria in Africa from which France and its colonies were administered during the time of the Nazi occupation of France. Modern France was founded after legendary French President, Charles Josef Marie De Gaulle(then an Army officer) led the French Resistance during World War II against Nazi Germany and established the Provisional French Government and led it from 1944-46 to re-establish democracy in France. Gualle died at Eglesias in France.

The Increasingly Assertive Russian Bear

With regard to Russia, Russian President Vladimir Putin some years back followed in the footsteps of his Chinese counterpart Xi Jinping and rubber-stamped himself into a lifetime President and won an bogey of an election in which carousel voting was routine much to the consternation of his political rivals and the international community spearheaded by his top political rival and bete noire Alexei Navalny. To critics, Mr. Putin has this to say"I work hard, listen to people, I am not a Czar". Obviously, Mr. Putin conveniently forgets he won a skewed mandate. The Russian Prime Minister Dmitri Medvedev who some years back warned the United States of an economic war if it went ahead with economic sanctions on Russia which anyway the United States did, recently gave way to Mr.Mikhail Mishustin. Incidentally, Makhail Gorbachev, architect of glasnost and perestroika in a bygone era is both reviled and revered in Russia today. Obviously, we need some perestroika in Putin's Russia today.

After the abdication of Czar Nicholas II at the turn of the century in the century that went by, the Bolshevik Revolution took place in Russia in 1917[the word Bolshevik in Russian means majority, their rivals were the Mensheviks or minority in Russian. The Bolsheviks won and the Mensheviks lost (Incidentally, 2017 was the centenary year of the Bolshevik Revolution.) Also, interestingly, although International Labour Day or May Day (which falls on May 1) is more associated with Russia, it has less to do with Russia and more to do with America. The significance of the day is that on May Day in 19th Century America at a gathering of the American Communist Party(of which, much later, the father of the atom bomb, Dr. Robert J Oppenheimer was a member, which led to his later side lining in the United States) in Chicago, the police opened fire which led to lot of bloodshed, May Day is observed to mark this sombre day) which saw the communist regime take over in Russia with Stalin as the first President of the Soviet Union(the word Soviet means collective farm in Russian, so U.S.S.R. means a Union of Collective Farms). The foreign policy of the Soviet Union under the General Secretary of the CPSU (Communist Party of the Soviet Union) who was also the President of the Soviet Union was, in its time, the most uniform one in the world. The 20th Century saw the dramatic rise of the Soviet Union in world politics and in the early days of its existence the Soviet Union used to throw lavish parties not unlike the social upstart who has gate crashed society. By the turn of the century, the Soviet Union had collapsed largely under the weight of its own sins, transgressions and excesses carried out with medieval demagogary combined with modern technology but also because the automatic workers revolution that Marx predicted never happened.

Soviet Successes

In its lifetime, the Soviet Union managed to pull off many spectacular successes, they being launching the world's first artificial satellite, the Sputnik(the size of a baseball) on Oct.24th,1956 that stunned the world, on a rocket derived from the R-7 Semyorka ICBM(better known as the Soyuz, a primitive ICBM by today's standards)(prompting Werner von Vandenburg, later responsible for America's moon landing success to remark "their Germans are better than ours" meaning whether it be the Americans or the Russians, it is the Germans in America or Russia who are powering either country's space successes) designed by senior scientist and rocket engineer Sergei Pavlovich Korolev who later was made a member of the Soviet Academy of Sciences and the Federal Space Agency. The Soviet Union also put the first man in space, Dr. Yuri Alexei Gagarin, on April 12, 1961 on a Vostok I vehicle [America put its first man in space, Alan Shepard exactly 23 days later, on May 5, 1961. Gagarin's death was shrouded in mystery for many years (the jury was out on this one, many conspiracy theories abounded for many years including a tampering of the oxygen vent on the Mig-15 that he and flight instructor, Vladimir Seryogin were flying) till the jury decided that probably Gagarin at the height of his fame took a swig of Vodka on that fateful day that sealed his and Seryogin's fate. People even reported hearing a big sound as Gagarin's aircraft crashed into a neighbouring hillock. There was also a 'crash' theory as a Su-15 was being tested at about the time that Gagarin's flight took off]. Gagarin was admired even by the West which described his description of the Earth as it went around the Sun as almost 'Keatsian' in description and said 'he was probably as the Russians claimed, the world's most universally loved man. Stalin was followed by Vladimir Illyvich Ullyanov Lenin and much of the 20th Century was absorbed by the rivalry or Cold War between the United States and the Soviet Union which in 1962 reached a crescendo and a boiling point during the Cuban Missile Crisis threatening to spill over into a Hot War when the then Soviet President, the wily and crafty Nikita Sergei Kruschev's extreme measure of placing missiles on America door step in Cuba(as per the Soviet narrative the U.S.S.R. did not have suitable ICBMs then) was met with stiff resistance by the then American President, the charismatic John.F.Kennedy who famously threatened nuclear annihilation in response. Fortunately, statesmanship and better sense prevailed, and the crisis was defused with Mr. Kruschev removing the missiles. Asked about the Chinese response to the crisis, the Chinese Ambassador to Cuba during the Cuban Missile Crisis, Wu Lengxi said "Of course, we did not support Kruschev's move, but we did not oppose it.". It is said a diplomat is a person who to hurl a stone says "Nice doggie". Likewise, the Chinese Ambassador's statement is a nuanced statement. By leaving out the word 'either' at the end of the statement, the Chinese Ambassador toned down China's opposition to Moscow's move.

The Soviet Union could not withstand the internal contradictions and the reign of terror that the Communist regime unleashed on its own people and in 1991 it imploded with the Soviet Union becoming dead as a country and from the dead weight that was the Soviet Union was born a nascent semi-autocratic democracy, Russia within a loose Commonwealth of Independent States(CIS) resembling the British Commonwealth(Headquarters-Marlboro House, London, Secretary General being Patricia Scotland) or the French Commonwealth(Organisation Internationales de la Francophonie with Michelle Jean, a former Governor General of Canada as its Secretary General). Member nations of the CIS include Ukraine, Kazhakastan, Belarus, Tajikistan, Turkmenistan, Kyrgystan, Azerbaijan, Uzbekistan etc and of course the 'Mother' country, Russia from whose womb all these "cousins" took shape. These new republics have split along East-West lines with countries like Ukraine and the Balkan nations like Rumania, Hungary, Serbia, Bosnia, Czech Republic, Slovakia, Herzogovnia and others jumping onto NATO and the West's bandwagon and these pro-West nations have been showing the proverbial zeal of new converts in shedding their Russian embrace, and others like Belarus, Azerbaijan and others have decided to stay put with their loyalty to Russia and the Russian 'Orbit'. India and Pakistan have been admitted to the select club Shanghai Cooperation Organisation as whose members Russia, China, India and Pakistan are cooperating.

Russian *and* the West's Intrigue-The New 'Cold War'

Russian 'murder' and intrigue in Ukraine's Crimea (which it annexed) and Georgia and South Ossetia and scores of other countries (not to speak of the West's own intrigue led by the United States) along with the Russian Super Weapons which it unveiled recently have compounded the mix and bedevilled relations between the Eagle and the Bear and unleashed a new 'Cold War'. But, yes, the Cold War as we knew it in the 20th Century is long since over. Instead, this has been replaced by a new common enemy 'Terrorism' (esp. after 9/11) with even the two Super Powers cooperating on this front. However, an important point. Global terrorism, of late, has been rather on the wane (Osama bin Laden and Saddam Hussein are long since dead, also witness the tenuous peace agreement that was cobbled together between the Taliban and the West led by America with America with the West agreeing to a proportionate and phased troop with drawl from Afghanistan beginning 2014 contingent on the Taliban sticking to its part of the agreement. Iraq has also more or less simmered down. However, things were bought to a boil by the killing of Iran's Quassem Soleimani by America in a drone strike. Also, Syria, where Russia used Sarin gas, continues to simmer on. Of course, outstanding and famous prickly points like the Israeli-Palestinian conflict which is supposed to be longest running conflict in the world are there, all sacrificed on the bedrock and anvil of Israeli and Arab instrasigience. In the Indian Sub-Continent, one has only to zero in on Pak terror to drive the point home that extremism and terror are still realities we have to contend with. On Pak, Pakistan seems to be forever waddling off and on the UN Financial Action Task Force(FATF, an organisation which has 39 members, its official languages being French and English)'s "grey" list of countries supporting terror alongwith countries such as Turkey and Malaysia(the inclusion of these two countries may surprise many) which are worse off ending up in the "black" list. The current President of the FATF Dr.Marcus Pleyer of Germany who succeeded Xiangmin Liu of the Peoples Republic of China has 2022 again placed Pakistan in the "grey" list. Other Presidents of the FATF include the first President Marshall Billingslea, Paul Gordon who was also President of the UN Security Council, Jaun Manuel Vega Serrano and others. Then, there is volatile Africa (Mali for e.g.) where nobody knows what will happen next. These are some of the last vestiges of terror. As noted by this author in another place, there is enough political, economic and social dynamite in the world today to match its ample stocks of uranium, plutonium and T.N.T.

These are realities we cannot wish away).

Coming back to Russia, the demise of the Soviet Union saw the eclipse of Russia as a world power. But, yes, Russia was, is and always will be a factor in several equations. Also, Russia has joined the quartet of emerging economies, India, Russia, China, Brazil and South Africa, BRICS which is beginning to punch much above its traditional weight in international politics and economics.

The Kremlin

Later Soviet Presidents include Nikita Sergei Kruschev, the long standing Leonid Brezhnev, the short lived tenures of Yuri Andropov and Constantin Chernenko and of course the brain behind glasnost and perestroika, Mikhail Sergei Gorbachev who along with America's Ronald Reagan (after numerous meetings including one on board the Russian cruise ship Maxim Gorky in neutral waters) were handed over the Peace Nobel for ending the Cold War. Prime Ministers included Bulganin, Alexei Kosygin, Nikolai Tikhonov, Nikolai Ryzkov, Dmitri Ustinov and many, many others. Soviet Foreign Ministers include the longstanding Andrei Gromyko (Grim Gromyko to the West) who looked on in pained contempt as Kruschev stamped his boot on the table at the United Nations threatening to bury the West in response to the Cuban Missile Crisis. The first President of Russia today as we know it was the energetic Boris Yeltsin (who after three heart surgeries carried on like a 'demon') who was followed in the saddle by today's Vladimir Putin who himself is proving to be pretty longstanding despite his so-called 'commitment' to ensuring free and fair elections which have another connotation in semi-democratic, semi-authoritarian Russia.

The Ministries

The precursor to the Russian Finance Ministry was the Treasury Governing Body founded by Czarina Catherine I later Catherine the Great who is counted among the ten greatest Queens in the World ranking third. However, the Russian Finance Ministry as we know it today was founded by Czar Alexander. The incumbent Russian Finance Minister is Anton Germanovich Siluanov who was preceded by Alexei Leonodovich Kudrin. The Russian Deputy Finance Minister is Tatyana Gennadovna. Russian Foreign Ministers include the first two Ivan Viskovatyi and Andrei Vassilyev during the Tsardom of Russia, then followed a scrum of Foreign Ministers from Nikita Pankin to Alexander Vorontsov. Among numerous others there were Leon Trotsky, Boris Panin, Vacheslav Molotov, the long standing Soviet Foreign Minister Andrei Gromyko, Eduard Shevardnadze (who became Georgia's First President on Georgia's independence), Andrei Kozyrev, Yevgeny Primakov, Igor Ivanov and the incumbent Sergei Lavrov. Russian Defence Ministers include the present Sergei Kuzhuzetovich Shoigu who is also the Chairman of the Council of Defence Ministers of the Commonwealth of Independent States (CIS) who is preceded in the post by Sergei Ivanov, Anatoliy Serdyukov and others Russian Deputy Defence Ministers include Dmitri Ustinov, Sergei Rybkov, Oleg Ostapenko who was a Commander-in-Chief of the Russian Space Forces as well as Director of ROSCOSMOS, the Russian Space Agency and the incumbent Alexander Fomin. The Russian Interior Minister is Vladimir Kolkolotsev. A former Deputy Foreign Minister is Vladimir Alexandrovich Popovkin, a former ROSCOSMOS Chief as well as a member of the Russian Academy of Sciences as well as the Federal Space Agency. The Russian Energy and Oil Minister is Alexander Valentinovich Novak who in a recent reshuffle was promoted to Deputy Prime Minister and Nikolay Shulginov was appointed Energy Minister in oil rich Russia. The Russian Agriculture Minister is Dmitri Patrushev and the Economy Minister is Maxim Oreshkin preceded by Maxim Reshetnikov.

The Chinese Panda

With regard to the Chinese Panda, the question as to what China is like is perhaps the most frequently asked question in the West. The demise of the Soviet Union (whom the Chinese call revisionists) saw the emergence of China as a factor in several equations as former Foreign Secretary Nirupama Rao put it. Actually, China has always been a great land power. China, has of late, emerged as a 'pole' in international relations. The rivalry between the United States and Communist China (which has all but in words given up Communism and embraced 'Capitalism') has intensified esp. in the trade field, witness the recent tit-for-tat tariffs and reverse tariffs being slapped by Washington and Beijing. Apart from the United States and Russia, Communist China is perhaps the only other power in the world which can assemble and deploy its military forces at a moment's notice anywhere in the world, with the attendant implications. The trade war has also forced China to open a lifeline with countries like India (witness the Wuhan Summit between Modi and XI Jinping) and Germany with whom it warmed up to the Germany 4.0 model.

Xi Jinping's Four Comprehensives

The Chinese President Xi Jinping's (who also chairs the Central Military Commission which is China's monolith of a Defence Ministry) 'four comprehensives'-

1. How to comprehensively develop China into a moderately prosperous country by 2022 which is on its way to becoming a reality soon.

2. How to comprehensively govern the party and the country strictly according to law and order.

3. How to develop China into an advanced socialist country by 2049, the Centenary year of the founding of the People's Republic of China etc

are postulates which have been codified into the Chinese Constitution.

Xi, the Core Leader and Mao Dse Dung

Xi, the Core Leader, follows in the footsteps of Mao Dse Dung, whose four 'modernisations' have also been codified into the Chinese Constitution, and is now treated on par with Mao. Other Chinese leaders whose theories have been taken note of are the first President Zhou En Lai, Deng Xiaoping Jiang Zemin and Xi's predecessor, Hu Jintao, a hydraulic engineer by profession, with his 'Scientific Outlook on Development'.

China's Belt and Road Initiative(BRI)
China has now embarked on the its ambitious One Belt One Road (OBOR) Project or Belt and Road Initiative spanning four continents Asia, Africa, Europe and Australia covering 60,000km which is some sort of a Modern Silk Road traversing parts of the traditional Silk Route (for which China views the South China Sea as a extension of its sea lanes based at Hainan Island on the Pacific Seaboard) and embarked on a 'cheque book diplomacy' in the Third World esp. Africa, a continent whose development has galvanised the Chinese economy, bankrolling as many as 28 economies all for strategic heft and political leverage. But the 'cheque book diplomacy' could bounce and in the event of the debtors' default how strong are the Chinese shock absorbers. The Belt and Road Initiative has rankled the nerves of countries like India and Germany[as expressed by former German Ambassador to India Dr. Martin Ney (current Ambassador being Walter Johannes Lindner)] which view it with grave misgivings, while countries like Morocco and, of course, Pakistan back it. Further, Pakistan, which is a collapsed economy and is on life support by the Chinese with the Chinese financing the CPEC (China Pakistan Economic Corridor) esp. the stretch all across Xinjiang bordering Pakistan and Afghanistan right up to the Gwadar port (which India has said is no threat) in South Pakistan opening up to the Arabian Sea much to the dismay of India. But, India should, and is supporting the Bangladesh, Myanmar, India China Corridor (BMIC) a strategy which will work to its advantage. In the Gulf too, the West led by the United States could become less dependant on Gulf oil as new oil deposits are found in the US and Canada and new oil technologies like fracking and horizontal drilling are discovered and China will begin to fill in the vacuum left by the West much to the chagrin, dismay and consternation of India. But, the new India West Asia Europe trade route could sound the deathknell for China's BRI and ground it even as Chinese investors pump and dump money in every country that hates China.
The Three Gorges Dam

China's planners have always been known to undertake giant projects. Take the case of the famous Three Gorges Dam spanning the Yangtze, China's 'Mother River' for centuries known for its deluges which wrought untold misery on the Chinese people. Then, Chinese planners thought of a way of damming the river and taming it. So was born the famous Three Gorges Dam, named after its three famous Gorges-Xiling, Wu and Qutang, one of the largest hydropower projects in the world, overlooking the city of Sandouping, Yiling District, Yichang Province, China and the gravity dam as it is called has an installed capacity of 25,500Mg Watts. In 2014, the dam produced a record 98.1 terra watt hours (TWh) of electricity and held the world record till the record was capped by Paraguay's Itaipu(Presa De Itaipu) Dam, another great hydropower dam damming the waters of the Parana on the border between Brazil and Paraguay which generated a whopping till now unsurpassed record of 103.1TWh of electricity.

Also, nowhere has the rise of China been met with such alarm than Japan, traditionally the 'Jewel of Asia' which has hit the alarm button.

The Mandarin's Power Pyramid-The Inner Clique

Chinese Finance Ministers include the incumbent Liu Kun, his predecessor Xiao Jie, the world famous Luo Jiwei who was sacked and replaced by the docile and pliable Xie Xuren in a country that frowns on dissent and ambition, Jin Renquing and others. Chinese Defence Ministers, Gen. X, Vice Chairman of the Central Military Commission and member, CMC include the inaugural holder Marshall Deng Pehui(1954-1959), the ambitious Marshall Lin Biao(whose aircraft was reportedly shot down in what were obscure circumstances over Orkhotsk, Mongolia as he attempted to flee a botched coup attempt against Mao with his family killing him and his family instantly), Marshall Ye Jianying, Marshall Xu Xiangquang, Gen. Geng Biao, Gen Zhang Aiping, Gen. Qin Jiewei, Gen. Chi Haotian, Gen Cao Gangchuan, Gen. Liang Guanglie, Gen. Chang Wanquan and the present one Wei Fenghe who helms the PLA and oversees China's Space Program.

In a country with a dual set up for its armed forces, the first Chief of General Staff is Marshall Su Yu followed by others such as Gen. Feng Fenghui, Gen. Chi Haotian, Gen Liang Guanglie, Gen. Chang Wanquan and the incumbent Gen. Huang Shu Kuang. The Chinese Minister of Civil Affairs and Public Security, State Councillor and Party Secretary and Minister of Supervision with top Police Officer rank of Police Commissioner General, a key portfolio in a Communist and authoritarian country like China with the State's all pervasive rigid gaze over the citizenry of the country, is Zhou Kezhi, deputy Ministers include Meng Hongwei, Wang Xiaohong, Shi Jun and others. Zhou Kezhi's predecessor Minister of Civil Affairs, State Councillor, Minister of Supervision, and Party Committee Deputy Secretary of the Central Commission for Discipline Inspection was Huang Shuxian(a former Minister of the Interior along with Li Liguo before the Ministry was disbanded). Incidentally, the first Minister of Public Security (1955-59) Chief of PLA Staff during the Sino-Indian War of 1962 who secured for China a key victory in the War (when neither country's Air Force or Navy was involved, a sore point with many Indian military officers who say had we sent our bombers and fighters to flatten Chinese troops, the outcome of the war would have been different) was Gen. Luo Ruishing(who died in Heidelberg, Germany), the architect of China's police and security apparatus. Chinese Foreign Ministers include the famous Li Zhaozing, Qian Qichen, Yang Jiechi, now a State Councillor and the incumbent Wang Yi who is also a State Councillor.

<u>The Apex</u>

In a country that still views the West through the Opium Wars prism and vice versa past Chinese Presidents include the legendary Mao Tsetung who once famously and, notoriously I should say, said "power flows out of the barrel of a gun" but who is still a master in statecraft and in whose War in the early 20th Century (1928 to be precise) another legendary figure, the good Indian doctor, Dr. Dwarkanath Kotnis made his now famous contribution. Dr. Kotnis's family and descendants are still treated as State guests in China.

The first Chinese Premier Zhou En Lai who took over in 1949(who once was in a brazenly affable mood at a Third World Conference as speaker after speaker went on to denounce Communism as just another form of colonialism. Mr. En Lai weathered it all, quite shamelessly I should say.) soon after the founding of the People's Republic of China (its difficult to say how things would have turned out had pro-democracy advocate Sun-Yat Sen not died in 1925). Chinese Presidents include Chiang-Kai-Shek who once famously told Nixon "India is bottomless pit" for its penchant to eat up whatever financial and food grain assistance that is given. However, once should say, today's India has given the answer that Chiang-Kai-Shek's statement deserves as famines have long since have become dead as a Dodo in India and India today is a rising world power which is also the reason for the current (2020) Chinese restiveness on the border. Other important Chinese Presidents include Liu Shiuxiu (during the 1962 Sino-Indian War), Jiang Zemin, Deng Xiao Ping who once called Rajiv Gandhi "Welcome, my young friend" when the latter came calling on him, the incumbent Xi Jinping's predecessor Hu Jintao, a hydraulic engineer by profession, and of course the present Xi Jinping who has achieved the same stature as Mao who 2019 fortified his position by becoming China's 'lifetime' President which China's rubber-stamp Parliament, the National People's Congress rubber-stamped(with all but 2 abstentions out of the total 4,800 delegates present and voting) apart from many, many others. Noted Chinese Prime Ministers include the incumbent Li Keqiang, Wen Jiabao, the butcher of Tiannanmen Li Peng and numerous others.

Other important Ministers include Commerce Minister Zhong Shan who was born in Shanyu County, Zhejiang Province in October,1955, Vice -Minister for Foreign Affairs and former Chinese Ambassador to India and Pakistan Luo Zhaohui (immediately before the incumbent Chinese Ambassador to India Sun Weidong), Vice-Minister in the International Department of the ruling Communist Party of China (CPC), Guo Yezhou. Incidentally, China's Commerce Ministry was known before 2003 as the Ministry of

Foreign Trade and Economic Cooperation (MOFTEC) and since 2003 it has been known as the Commerce Ministry of China. There are interesting but rather macabre examples of the Chinese concept of social responsibility. Once in what is a true story, a Chinese father, when faced with a socially deviant son, turned him over to the authorities and the authorities came and shot him dead and the grief-stricken father was the one who cried the loudest. However, such stories could be a little dated in today's China as China grapples with a new reality, but such stories still ring true. China is also one of the few countries in the world today where age is still treated with respect and incidentally, India's icon Rabindranath Tagore who became the first Asian to win the Nobel Prize when he won the Literature Nobel in 1913 has a large following in China and film stars Aamir Khan and Rajnikant draw a small scrum.

II

Jewel of Asia

'Jewel of Asia'-The Japanese Political System

Nowhere has the rise of China rankled nerves than in Japan. Japan, a constitutional monarchy like Britain, Sweden or much of Scandinavia or the Nordic countries or many other countries of the world like Thailand and other countries, is unitary in structure. During the Imperial Period the Prime Minister was appointed by the Emperor and did not need confirmation from the Diet, the Japanese Parliament. But now the Prime Minister is appointed by the Emperor after being designated by the Diet following which he must take a vote of confidence from the Diet. After that, the Prime Minister appoints 19 Ministers known as Ministers of State. Only the Prime Minister can dismiss the Ministers. The Cabinet is collectively responsible to the Diet and must resign if a motion of no-confidence is passed against it.

Japanese Prime Ministers include the first Prime Minister during the Imperial Period, Ito Hirobumi who entered office in 1885, first Japanese Prime Minister during the Non-Imperial Period, Katsura Taro, Takeo Miki. Takeo Fukuda, Admiral Keisuke Okada, Yoshihiro Miri, General Hideki Tojo who was executed as a war criminal at the end of World War-II by the U.S.Army MP's on 12/23/1948 at Army built gallows in Sugamo Prison, Tokyo and who was also Japan's Education, Science and Technology, Culture and Sports Minister and Minister for Education Rebuilding, Inukai Tsuyoshi who was born on June 5th, 1855 and was at the helm from 1931-32 and who was assassinated by 11 young naval officers on May 15, 1932, Toshiki Kaifu, Tomichi Murayama, Ryutaro Hashimoto, Keizo Obuchi, Yoshihiro Mori, Junichiro Koizumi of the Komeito Party who said of India following the spate of economic reforms unleashed by the Narasimha Rao Government and the subsequent Indian economic recovery "Now we to start looking this way too", Yasuo Fukuda, Taro Aso who was also Japan's Deputy Prime Minister(the Deputy Prime Minister also handles the Economic Cooperation with Russia portfolio and also helms the Ministry for ensuring Industrial Competetiveness and Finance Minister, Yukio Hatoyama, Naoto Kan, Yoshihiko Noda, Shinzo Abe(of the Liberal Democratic Party) who has the longest incumbency among Japan's post-War Prime Ministers serving for three straight consecutive terms and who courted India the most among world leaders as India slowly enters the Global Big League among the world's economic powers and becomes a economic powerhouse in its own right, Yoshihide Suga who is a former Cabinet Secretary[other beaurucrats include Vice Minister for Foreign Affairs Takeo Akiba{a post akin to Foreign Secretary}(who is well versed in international affairs, esp. Oceanic Affairs)] and who entered office in 2021, the incumbent Fumio Kishida and a galaxy of other distinguished Japanese Prime Ministers who live in the *Kantei* or Prime Minister's residence.

The Emperor

The Japanese Emperor is Naruhito who along with his Empress Nakasone paid homage at the mausoleums of his great, great grandparents after he ascended the Chrysanthemum throne. In Japan, only male heirs can be anointed Emperor. His predecessor Emperor was Akihito who was preceded by Emperor Hirohito(or Emperor Showa of the Showa dynasty). Other Japanese Emperors include Emperor Konoe during the 19th Century, the first Emperor, Emperor Jimmu who existence is thought to be mythical and a host of other revered Emperors.

The Cabinet

The Ministers of State

One of the most important Japanese Ministries is the Ministry of the Interior housed in the 2-1-2, Common Government Building, Kamusugaseki, Chiyoda-ku, Tokyo, Japan. The various Ministers of the Interior and Communications include Seiko Noda, Ministers of State for Interior and Communications Shinsuke Okuno and Manabu Sakai, Senae Takayichi, Masashiko Shibayama and others.

Foreign Ministers include Toshimitsu Motegi, Taro Kono and others.

Defense Ministers include Taro Kono etc.

Finance Ministers include as noted earlier, former Prime Minister and Deputy Prime Minister Taro Aso and others.

The Ministers of Education, Science and Technology, Culture, Sports and Education Rebuilding include Masashiko Ishida, Yoshimasa Hayashi, Hideki Tojo, the present Minister Masuo Fujio and others.

The important Justice Ministers include Cheiko Nohno, Keiko Chiba, Eisaku Moro, Keishu Tanaka, Yoko Kamikawa(who as Japan's Justice Minister gave the death sentence to the accused in the Tokyo Metro massacre case), Horoshi Hiraguchi, the present Justice Minister Masako Mori and others. It is noteworthy here that women have made rapid inroads in the largely male bastion that is Japan. For e.g. in 2017, Ryoko Azuma was appointed the Commander of the Japanese helicopter borne warship, Izuma. But, yes, these are largely symbolic gains and Japan continues to be a male bastion.

Agriculture, Fisheries and Animal Husbandry Ministers include the present Minister Taku Eto, his predecessor Ken Saito and others.

Economy, Industries and Trade Ministers include the present Hiroshi Kajiyama, Hiroshige Seko, former Prime Minister Junichiro Koizumi's suave, dappling and charismatic son Shinjiro Koizumi who now heads the Environment Ministry and others.

As noted now, Shinjiro Koizumi is the Environment Minister and as Japan's Environment Minister Shinjiro Koizumi, at a international meeting 2021 called for the reduction of greenhouse houses consequent upon the Paris climate agreement.

A former Cabinet Secretary(who is also the Minister for mitigating the impact of the U.S. bases in Okinawa) is the present Prime Minister Yoshihide Suga.

Japanese political parties include apart from the Liberal Democratic Party, the Komeito Party of former Japanese Prime Minister Junichiro Koizumi and others.

Japanese Vice-Minister for Foreign Affairs(a post akin to Foreign Secretary) is Takeo Akiba(an expert in international affairs esp. Oceanic Affairs). His predecessor is Shinsuke. J. Sugiyama(currently Japanese Ambassador to United States) and before him Vice-Minister for Foreign Affairs was Kenichiro Sasae(who was Ambassador to United States before Sugiyama). Incidentally, Kenichiro Sasae, who is now retired, was close to former U.S. President Donald Trump's son-in-law Jared Kushner who was Trump's advisor.

Given the pacifist disposition of post-War Japan, there are interesting examples of the Japanese approach to war. For instance, there was a case of a Japanese Emperor who when faced with the prospect of war solved it with deftness and finesse by sending an emissary to the opposing General(a spiritually realized man who understood the futility of war) who accepted the olive branch and then there was no war. Perhaps Japanese jingoism during World War-II was an anomaly. Whatever, the world should accept Japanese(and German) pacifism with more than a pinch of salt as Japanese and indeed the world's history is full of wars nobody thought would happen and such instances are few and far in between and all is touch and go and Japan(along with Germany which are two 'candidate nuclear powers') could pick up arms again and the world should be wary of these two giants. But, a caveat here. Whether atom-bombed Japan which is pacifist to a point will pick up arms again is an open-ended question and so also Germany which has wizened up to a despotic, criminal and autocratic leader who has more than a sting in his tail helming it will go belligerent does seem like a long shot. But new flashpoints have emerged and the world is grappling with a Molotov cocktail. It does never seem to be spared of them.

III

Western Europe

Germany-A Political Analysis

The first German Chancellor was *der Kanzler* Otto von Bismarck who took office in 1871 and who was followed by a host of German Chancellors like Paul und von Hindenburg who ruled not just Germany but occupied lands south of Prussia as far as up to Alsace, France, the double-dealing Hatchet man with a sting in his tail as noted earlier Adolf Hitler under whom on 1 September, 1939 as Hitler was receiving the Polish Foreign Minister German bombs fell on Poland and so began World War-II, following the fall of the Third Reich or Nazi Germany, founder of *modernisches Deutschland* or modern Germany Konrad Adenuar established modern Germany, Adenuar was followed by Kurt George Wiesinger(1963-66), Walter Scheel(1966-67), Heinrich Lubcke, Erhard Wilhelm Ludwig of the Christian Social Union(CSU), Willy Brandt of the CSU who helmed Germany from 1967-1974, Helmut Kohl, a one time German Finance Minister and President of Rhineland Palatinate State, Helmut Schmidt who served as Defense Minister and Finance Minister and was G-8's President in 1985 and 1992, Gerhard Furth Kurt(1996-2005)

Schroeder whose most important political project was Agenda 2010 and led the SDP in an alliance with the Greens, the present *die Kanzlerin* of the German powerhouse which is Europe's largest economy and fourth largest economy in the world just behind the United States, China and Japan, Angela Merkel who is on far fewer cards than before after the SDP(Social Democrats), a pan European party forced a coalition on her party the Christian Democratic Party(Miss Merkel is on on far weaker footing now than ever before conceding key ministries such as Finance, Foreign, Interior to the SDP) for her to stay in power. Such are the vagaries of electoral fortunes as Frau Merkel(whose spouse is Herr Joachim Sauer), once seen as one of the most powerful women in the world, sees her power and influence increasingly being chipped away in what is a more organic, natural, scientific and logical reflection of the German scenario. But then she has won her place in history leaving her indelible footprint in the annals of German and World history. So it is that another 'loveless' coalition continues to hold sway in Berlin with the firebrand 'Jusos' or youth wing of the SDP breathing down the neck of the senior leadership of the SDP to ensure that Miss Merkel sways to the tunes of the senior leadership of the SDP. They will be a 'thorn' in the flesh of party President Andrea Nahles and other senior members not to mention Miss Merkel. This is, of course, not an exhaustive list of all the German Chancellors.

Coming to the German Presidents, the first President was Friedrich Ebert of the SDP (4th Feb. 1871 to 28th February, 1925) who entered office in 1919 but died midway into his Presidency in office in 1925. Ebert was followed by Theodore Heuss and Paul und von Hindenburg who was pressurized by Hitler to declare the latter Chancellor although the Nazis were in a minority in the Nazi Parliament, the Reichstag. This shows the Nazis never really had the tacit sanction and approval of the people of Deutschland. A point to note about German Presidents and Vice-Chancellors is that some of the Chancellors served terms as Presidents and since 1969 often the Foreign Minister has doubled up as Vice-Chancellor(a post akin to Deputy Prime Minister in other parliamentary systems) including the present Foreign Minister Heiko Mass who is currently serving a concurrent term as Vice-Chancellor. Heinrich Lubke became the first President after the fall of the Third Reich in 1945. Other German Presidents include Roman Herzog, Erich von Weiszacker, Walter Scheel, Klaus Kinkel, Johannes Rau, Horst Kohler, Egon Franke, Karl Christerns, Jurgen Mollerman, Hans Dietrich Genschner, Joshka Fisher, John Guack, Foreign Minister and Vice-Chancellor Guido Westervelle(he was Vice-Chancellor in Miss Merkel's second cabinet from 2005 to 2008.) who died of Parkinsons, the present President Frank Walter Steinmeir, a one time Foreign Minister and others.

German Vice-Chancellors include the first, Franz Bluche, Herman Goring, Guido Westerville, the incumbent, Foreign Minister Heiko Maas and others.

German Finance Minister Olaf Scholz(now *der Kanzler* or Chancellor) was SDP party President before he took over as Finance Minister. So, the 2017 German Government is a continuation of the same coalition of 2013 for Deutschland. The German Chancellor is elected by direct popular for a period of 4 years through a curious admixture of the Westminister form of parliamentary democracy and is responsible to the Bundestag. Elections are due this year(2021) but as of August nothing seems to have come of it. However, Germany may see a regime change shortly with the lameduck government of Chancellor Merkel(Chancellor since 2004 when she came to power through a by-election, although she served a earlier stint as Chancellor) giving way to a new government. The latest on this is that German Elections have been held Oct 2021 and Finance Minister the anti-immigrant Olaf Scholz(who contrary to initial expectations is likely to introduce immigrant friendly policies as he rings in a new German Government) has been elected the new German *der Kanzler* or Chancellor defeating Minister Prasidant(Minister President or Premier) of North Rhineland Region Armin Laschet[also Christrian Democratic Union (CDU) President] for whom it was a game of Chancellor or bust and he chose to go bust. Mr.Scholz has since taken charge. Senior Ministers in Chancellor Scholz's Cabinet include Finance Minister Christian

Lindner, Interior Minister Nancy Faeser, Defense Minister Christine Lambrecht and Foreign Minister Annalena Baerboek who together from the kitchen Cabinet of Mr.Scholz. First German Finance Minister is Adolf von Scholz and Volker Bouffier is Minister Prasident of Germany's southern Hesse State while the late Thomas Schaefer was Finance Minister of Hesse State before he committed suicide by jumping before a running train due to Covid-19 worries leaving behind a shell-shocked nation. Incidentally, Germany's financial capital, Frankfurt, is in Hesse State. And Markus Thomas Theodore Soeder is Minister Prasident of southern Bavaria State and President of the Christian Social Union(CSU), the CDU's southern sister. Interior Minister Horst Seehofer in Merkel's government, a conservative hardliner who is not a minister but a conservative old hand whose sympathies seem to lie with slogans like *'Kinder, stadt Inder'*(Children, not Indians) has proved to be Miss Merkel's migraine. Then, another source of worry is the far-right Alternative for Germany which cornered 30% of seats in the present Bundestag as far-right parties made deep inroads in not just Germany but all across Europe in countries such as Italy, Austria(where it was part of the mainstream until recently), not to mention France where, in what was a shell-shocker of an election for Europe, far-right leader Marine Le Pen almost became the President of France and other countries. Right wing parties like the National Socialist Underground and the Alternative for Germany also held demonstrations against immigrants in German cities such as Chemnitz etc. Frau Merkel, of course, toes a more tolerant line towards immigrants reigning in the hardliners. The CDU's southern sister Party the Christian Social Union in conservative southern states like Bavaria(where post-1945 unheard of racist authoritarian policies are followed) is another fly in Frau Merkel's tea cup. The storm in a tea cup, the Melanin pigment, obviously seems to matter a lot to Europeans. A sort of a reverse colonial hangover that is present in India. We are here referring to the undercurrent of fascination for white skin that is present in India, something which is not there anywhere else in the world, neither in Africa, nor in

China nor for that matter to some extent in that melting pot, America. The only saving grace seems to be Foreign Minister Heiko Mass(a former Justice Minister) who adopts a tough approach towards the more radical elements and the views of Defense Minister Annegret Kramp Karenbauer are a '?' although former Defense Minister Ursula Gertrud von Der Leyen(a former Women and Child Development Minister) is seen as a moderate. But their influence could be tempered by the youth wing of the SDP who are a nightmare for not only the senior leadership of the SDP but by implication even the German government. Indeed a sobering thought. Indeed a very, very sobering thought. Young blood is definitely hot. Other Foreign Ministers include Sigmar Gabriel and others. This sums up German politics *kurz and klar*.

Right turn in Italy too

Recently(2020), Italy got a new Prime Minister, Mario Draghi. The right-wing dispensation of former Italian Prime Minister Guiseppe Conte who headed a coalition of a clutch of parties comprising of the Northern League, the anti-establishment Five Star Movement, Forza Italy(Go Italy) of former Prime Minister, the powerful and influential but scandal-tainted Silvio Berlusconi(known for his *banga, banga* sex scandals), the Centre-right and other parties had kept Italy largely out of the Centre-left or socialist orbit. Under the new administration of Prime Minister Mario Draghi Italy may swing towards a more accommodative and less radical ideological posture. Other political parties in Italy include the Liberals, Centrists and others. The Italian President is Sergio Matarella. Interestingly, Moody's recently ranked big power Italy(baa-) below India(baa or lower medium) and the two countries are at par with countries like Phillipines, Bulgaria, Columbia and others in terms of economic performance. India finished ahead of Italy as the sixth largest financial arrangement in the world dead heat and breathing down the neck of even the UK which ranks among the Big-5. There could be a photo finish here for the fifth spot.

The upgrade came nearly after nearly 13 years during the tenure of the Modi I government(Congress misrule?). But, then, Covid-19 interfered and only now India and the world are recovering their feet. The Italian Prime Minister ranks fourth in the Italian order of precedence and is known as the President of the Council of Ministers and must receive a vote of approval from the Council to take decisions. The position is similar to most other parliamentary systems except that the Italian Prime Minister cannot request dissolution of Parliament or dismiss Ministers. Italian Prime Ministers include the first Count Camilo Benso Conte Di Cavour of the Kingdom of Italy, Giovanni Lanza, Alessandro Fortis. Francisco Crispi, Antonio Salandra, Guiseppe Pella, Mariano Rumor, Luigi Di Facta, Aldo Moro, Bettino Craxi, the longest serving Italian Prime Minister, the ludicrous figure Benito Mussolini, Guilio Andreotti, Romano Prodi, Giuliano Amato, Silvio Berlusconi, Mario Monti, Matteo Renzi, the man with a velvet touch, Paulo Gentiloni, Guiseppe Conte, as noted earlier the incumbent Mario Draghi and many, many others. Italian Kings include Victor Emmanuel III(who removed Mussolini and thereby became the Messiah of the Italian people) during World War II and others. However, Italy is no longer a monarchy.

Italian Interior Ministers include Giovanni Lanza, Antonio Salandra, Alesandro Fortis, Mariano Rumor, Francisco Crispi, Guiseppe Pella, Luigi Di Facta, Marco Minetti, Matteo Salvini, the present Luciana Lamorgese and numerous others. The Italian Ministry of Economic Development, a rather key ministry, has been called by different names under different administrations during different time periods like the Ministry of Economy and Finances, Ministry of Commerce, Industry, Crafts and Trade, Ministry of Commerce and Industry, Ministry of Crafts and Industries, the Ministry of Economic Development and Crafts etc. Spread over the years, the various Ministers of Economic Development as the Minister is currently called include Guiseppe Togni, Giovanni Tria, Silvio Gava, Guilio Andreotti, Federica Guidi, Paulo Romano, Romano Prodi, Mario Monti,Silvio Berlusconi Matteo Renzi, Paulo

Gentiloni, Carlo Calenda, Luigi Di Maio of the Northern League, Stefano Pataonelli, the present Minister Giancarlo Giorgetti and many others. In these times of Gender Equality, glass ceilings and political correctness Italy too has made provision for a Minister of Equal Oppurtunities and one concerned former Minister was former showgirl Mara Carfagna. The Vice-President of the influential industrial lobby Confidustria is Antionella Mansi. As far as Prime Ministers go, the controversial Italian Prime Minister, Benito Mussolini was really a ludicrous figure in European politics, although the millions of Italians who suffered under him had nothing to be happy about. For e.g. at the start of World War II, Mussolini, with typical rhetoric threw his weight behind Hitler. However, in Africa and elsewhere, the Germans led by the legendary German General Erwin Rommel soon found out, Mussolini's troops were not the disciplined soldiers of ancient Rome, and the Germans had to extricate Mussolini's soldiers from one mess to another. Mussolini played havoc with Italian(and world) politics till King Victor Emmanuel III had him removed.

Former Italian Prime Ministerial candidates('Prime Ministers in waiting' to borrow a phrase from Indira Gandhi's lexicon) include Carlo Calenda, Marco Minetti, former European Commissioner, Margerethe Vesteger and others. Former Italian Prime Minister Mario Monti too is a former European Commissioner. The present European Commission President is Ursula von der Leyen who was preceded by Stella Kyriakidou, a Maltese psychologist, former Luxemborg Prime Minister Jean Claude Juncker, Jean Borosso and others. The European Commission consists of 27 members, each member holding one portfolio much like national ministers, with each European Commission being analogous to a national Ministry and each European Commissioner being analogous to a national minister. The European Trade Commissioner is Mairead McGuiness who was preceded by Phil Hogan, Cecilia Malmstorm, first Trade Commissioner Jean Ray and others. The European Commissioner for Internal Market is Thierry Breton and Dunja Mijatovic is the European Commissioner for the high profile Human Rights

Commission. Antonio Tajani is the European Parliament President and Donald Tusk is the European Union President. Tusk recently met ambassadors of Rumania, Hungary and other countries and sought their cooperation in relations with the European Union.

The Spanish Matador-Spain

Spanish Prime Ministers include the incumbent Pedro Sanchez Perez De Castejon, his predecessor Mariano Rajoy Brey who is a former Interior Minister of Spain, the first Prime Minister under the 1976 Constitution, Adolofo Gustavo Suarez, his predecessor, the last dictator, Ferdinand Franco and numerous others. Into his second term, Prime Minister Sanchez, belonging to the Spanish Socialist Workers Party of which he is the Secretary General(in 2013 he was deposed as Secretary General in a 'internal coup' only to be re-elected a year later in 2014) in his first term, headed a coalition of convenience of a group of rhinos and tigers, a most inorganic, unscientific and unholy alliance of parties like the Podemos, Ciudadanos and smaller parties united together by nothing more than the desire to come to power which they did by fall by passing a motion of no confidence against a stunned Prime Minister Brey of the PPP who went into the annals of Spanish history of Prime Ministers to be deposed so. In his second term, Prime Minister Sanchez who secured a wafer thin majority again came to power by fall through a key 18 abstentations by Basque separatists.

The incumbent President of Catalonia, a autonomous province of Spain that is seeking to break away from Madrid is Pere Aragones who is preceded by Quim Torra and Carles Puigdemont. On the topic of Catalonia's 'independence', it is worth noting that Senyor Puigdemont was arrested in Germany in 2019. The Catalonian President is addressed as El Molt Senyor(or The Honorable) and lives in the Casa De Canonges.

The incumbent Foreign Minister of Spain is Arancha Gonzales Sanchez and the Home Minister is Fernando Grande Marlaska. Other Home Ministers include Mariano Rajoy Brey, Luis Bravo

Gonzalez, Rafael Peres Ruis and others. The Spanish Secretary of State for Internal Security is Rafael Peres and the Spanish Home Ministry was founded in 1828.

The King of Spain, a constitutional Monarchy, is King Felipe VI. Other Spanish Kings include Ferdinand VII and others. Incidentally, Crown Princess Maria Theresa of Spain was one among a series of high profile Covid-19 deaths.

The Speaker of the Spanish Congress of Deputies or the lower house of the Spanish Parliament is Barcelona MP Meritxell Batet. Known as the 101 Cortez of Spain Senor Batet is one among a set of Speakers that include Ana Paulina Gonzalez and others. The Speaker is assisted in his duties by four Vice-Presidents. The 3rd Vice-President, for instance, is Luis Inacio Gonzalez.

The Swiss Confederacy

The President of the Swiss Confederation or the President of the Confederation or Colloquially as the President of Switzerland is the President of the 7 member Federal Council, Switzerland's executive branch. The officeholder is elected by the Federal Assembly for 1 year and is eligible for re-election but not immediately and chairs the meetings of the Federal Council and undertakes special representational duties.

The current officeholder is former Foreign Minister Ignazio Cassis elected on January 1, 2022. He was preceded by Guy Parmelin, Simmonetta Sommaruga, Ueli Maurer, Alain Berset, Doris Leuthord. Other officeholders include Joseph Buro, Adolf Ogi, Paul Migy and the first President, Jonas Furrer. The Presidential Palace is the Federal Palace although the President has two Palaces.

Portugal

The Portuguese Prime Minister is Luis Antonio De Costa GCIH. Lisbon's 118th Prime Minister, the epicenter of power, a lawyer by profession and a person who traces his origins to Goa, Mr. De Costa recently created a minor flutter in the Portuguese Parliament by asking MPs if the color of skin decided the type of questions to be asked. The Portuguese President is Marcelo Rebelo De Sousa who is preceded in the post by Anabil Cavaco Silva.

The Portuguese Leader of the Opposition is Rui Rio. Born on August 6th, Mr. Rio, a former Porto Mayor, became the Leader of the Opposition by bogarting 54.4 of Portuguese Opposition vote pie. He studied at the Porto's Deutsche Schule or Porto's German School and during his college days headed the only Communist Student's Union then existent in Western Europe.

Greece

The Prime Minister of the Greek Hellenic Parliament is Katerina Sakellaropolou who became Prime Minister 2020 by securing 129 votes. The Greek President is Kyriokos Mitsotakies and the Finance Minister is Christos Stykouros. Their corresponding predecessors were Prime Minister Alexis Tspiras, a one time Finance Minister who went down in a blaze of glory over the Greek bailout plan and President Prokopis Pavlopoulos. Former President Andreas Poupandrou played a pivotal role in Athen's politics during his time.

Austria

Austrian Chancellors include the present Chancellor Sebastian Kurz who at 33 yrs when he entered office is the youngest world leader, the first Chancellor Dr. Karl Renner, Reinhold Mitterlehner, Werner Faymann, Christian Kern, Dr. Briget Bierlien and others. Vice-Chancellors include the incumbent Werner Kogler who heads the Greens who are for the first time participating in Government not just in Austria but perhaps anywhere across the world in a arrangement termed 'exotic' by the Austrian media, Jodok Fink, Heinz Christian Strache, Christian Kern and others. Mr. Kogler is also a member of the National Council, Austria's Parliament. It is noteworthy that the Greens are making their presence felt in the

Austrian Parliament. For e.g. under Green pressure the government of Chancellor Kurz has declared it will make Austria carbon neutral by 2040 in the process making Austria the first carbon neutral country in the world. But, with the UN saying 2021 the world may miss the climate target, this deadline may have to be postponed. Among other goals that the Austrian government has adopted is something that is a residual effect of Mr. Kurz's former alliance with the far-right, a time when there was shot in the right arm in Austria -enforcing anti-immigration curbs, a topic that at once raises heat and din all across Western Europe what with Europe's colored 'kalediescopic' diaspora.

Austrian Interior Ministers include the incumbent Karl Nehammer, his predecessor Herbert Kickl(in the Kurz I government, a government that fell after the far-right pulled back support to Chancellor Kurz but not before cornering all the key ministries like Interior, Foreign and Finance leaving the puppet government of Kurz at their mercy. Not to be outdone, Mr. Kurz clung to power in a way best described by opposition leader Pamela Wagner as "a shameless example of clinging to power". However, that was a government that was doomed, a government that was living on borrowed time.) In the event, like so many politicians across the world, Mr. Kurz was 'vindicated' at the hustings winning a second term as Chancellor. The Speaker in the Kurz I Parliament was Doris Buro. Other Austrian Interior Ministers include former Austrian Chancellor Werner Faymann and others.

Far-right inroads into Austrian mainstream politics is nothing new. In 1,996, shocked and startled by the far-right's inroads into Austrian politics spearheaded by a popular upsurge, President Thomas Klejstil made his displeasure known to the then Austrian Chancellor and Austrian far-right leader Joerg Haider created a minor storm in Austria before he died in a road accident. The present Austrian President is Alexander van Der Bellen. The President's post is largely ceremonial although there have been times when the President has exercised his reserve powers to reign in belligerent Governments like during the time of Thomas Klejstil.

While on this topic, it is worth recalling that the Austrian Interior Minister under Chancellor Kurz(in the Kurz I Government) Herbert Kickl was part of the axis of the willing against immigrants along with German Interior Minister Horst Seehofer and the then Italian Interior Minister Matteo Salvini. Also, in the Kurz I Government the far-right was at the helm in most of the key Ministries such as Interior, Finance and Defense once again underscoring the far right's inroads in roads in European politics and life.

Going further back in Austrian history and politics, former Austrian Chancellor and Foreign Minister(during the 18th Century) Prince Klemens Wenzel Nepomuk Lothar von Matternich, Austrian diplomat and politician and Architect of European unity(it is his legacy that the European Union was handed over the 2012 Peace Nobel for making war unthinkable in Europe) has the world's longest incumbency as Foreign Minister. He was Foreign Minister from 1709 to 1748 and Chancellor from 1722 till the liberal revolutions of 1748 forced him out. Outwardly seen as nothing more than a aristocratic playboy, behind hidden doors in the counsels of Europe and the world he was carving out his place in history. In second place as the world's second longest serving Foreign Minister is former Saudi Foreign Minister(from 1975 till his death in 2015) Saud Al Salman bin Mohammed al Sati.

Ireland

The Irish Prime Minister currently Michael Martin, reports to the Irish President currently Michael. D. Higgins. Before Michael Martin the Irish Prime Minister was Leo Varadkar. The Irish Leader of the Opposition is Louise Mcdonald. She is the second female Leader of the Opposition and the first female Sinn Fein(political wing of the IRA) President to become Leader of the Opposition. She won by a margin of 53.3% of the votes polled. Peter McGuiness whose son was also involved in Sinn Fein activities was another prominent Sinn Fien President and IRA leader.

Scandinavia and the Cockpit of Europe

Finland-The Happy Country

The Finnish Prime Minister Sanna Mirella Marin is at 34 when she entered office the world's second youngest leader and the first woman to helm the country. She is preceded by Anti Juhani Rynni(only for 6 months), Juha Petri Sipila who after a successful stint in business entered politics, Jyrki Katainnen who survived a assassination attempt, Alexander Stubb, Mouno Koivisto, Urho Kaleva Kekkonen(the last two being also President with Kekkonen wielding an unusual amount of power and influence although he continues to be a popular figure in Finnish politics and life) and others. Finnish Presidents include the incumbent Sauli Vainamo Ninisto, Taaja Halonnen, the Prime Minister duo Urho Kaleva Kekkonnen and Mouno Koivisto, Karlo Juho Stalhberg and others.

Denmark

The Danish Prime Minister is Mette Fredriksson who is preceded by Lars-Lokke Larsmussen of the Center-Right Venstre Party who was at the helm from 2015-2020 and other Prime Ministers include Helle-Thorning Schmidt and others.

Like much of Europe and the world, many of the countries of Scandinavia and the Nordic Council are constitutional monarchies modelled on the British Westminster model and Denmark is no exception. The Danish Queen is Queen Margrethe II and 15th in the heir apparent line of succession is Crown Prince Fredrick.

Sweden

At the apex of the constitutional monarchy that Sweden is, is the Swedish King, currently Carl Gustaf Folke Herbertus(born April 30th, 1946) or Carl Gustaf XVI who ascended the Swedish throne on the ath of his grandfather Adolf Gustaf on 15th Sept.1973.

Louis De Geer the architect of the Swedish bicameral Riksdag(or Parliament) which replaced the centuries old Riksdag of the Estates in 1866 became the first Prime Minister of Sweden in 1876 and he was succeeded by a long succession of Prime Ministers that included Ingvar Karlsson, the assassinated Olof Palme (who in a bid to veer Sweden away from the West and Moscow served as one of the pillars of the Non-aligned Movement along with the Indian Prime Minister and the left-leaning former Tanzanian Prime Minister Julius Nyerere. Still on the topic of Super Power politics during the Cold War, it is worthy of note that some countries like India, China and to some extent countries like Vietnam and Egypt have always escaped all sorts of orbits and emerged as independent orbits in themselves with their own spheres of influence) the present Prime Minister, Kjell Stafan Lofven of the Social Democratic Party and others. Kjell Stefan Lofven was back in the saddle after a dicey inconclusive election in 2018 that threw up other Prime Ministerial hopefuls such as right wing opposition leader Ulf Kristersson who in fact was asked mid-2021 by Speaker Andrea Norlen of Lofven's Moderate Party to to take a vote but Lofven used the vote as a springboard to swing back to power. As the dice was rolled there were other hopefuls such as the far right Sweden Democrats with whom neither the right nor left wants to negotiate. The latest on this is that Anna Magdalena Johnsson has since charge as the PM of Sweden.

The Land of Straights,Bays and Fjords-Norway

Like Denmark and Sweden, Norway too is a constitutional monarchy and the Norwegian Queen and King are Queen Sonja and King Harold IV. The Norwegian Prime Minister, called Iron Erna after her former British counterpart Margaret Thatcher for her steely, tough but when necessary genteel demeanour is Erna Solberg.

Iceland

The Icelandic Prime Minister is Katrin Jakobsdottir who is preceded by Sigmundur Gunlogsson who is now a member of the Althing, the Icelandic Parliament. Iceland has a very long history as an independent country dating back to the time of the first Prime Minister Jon Magnusson of the Home Rule Party when Iceland was under Home Rule from Denmark much like Greenland is now. The Icelandic President is Gouni Thorlacius Johnnsson and lives in the Bessestoir, the Presidential Palace. Other Presidents include the first President Bjorn Svensson, Bjarni Benedictsson and others. And Sigmundur Runnarson is one of the members of the Althing.

Greenland

Greenland, under Home Rule from Denmark has a Westminister parliamentary form of Government where the Prime Minister is the head of government, the incumbent being Mute Bourup Egede of the Inuit Ataqatigiit Party who reacting to former US President Donald Trump's offer of US $100 million in gold for Greenland said Mr. Trump's offer made him realise how precious his homeland was. The offer is not new. Harry Truman made the same offer. Perhaps, the US has always wanted to polevault to the Arctic, with its attendant rich benefits. Mr. Egede is preceded in his position by the sixth Prime Minister of Greenland, Kim Kielsen(2014-2021) of the Siumut Party. Under Mr. Kielsen, a former mariner and police inspector with the Poliziet in Upernarik and Paamnik, the Deputy Prime Minister was Anda Uldum. Mr. Kielsen is preceded in the Premier's post by Aleqa Hammond, a member of the Folktieng, the Danish Parliament and leader of the Siumut. Mr. Kielsen is succeeded in the Siumut President's position by Erik Jensen, the present President and preceded by Aleqa Hammond. His deputy while Siumut President was Hans Enoksen. The first Prime Minister of Greenland was Jonathan Motzfeldt who soon became Prime Minister after Greenland gained Home Rule from Denmark. Since

Greenland is an autonomous territory of Denmark, the Greenlandic Sovereign is the Danish Sovereign Margrethe II. As regards the American Dream of buying Greenland, that may just remain remain a pipedream and end up a damp squib as successive Greenlandic administrations have made it clear Greenland was not up for sale and it would indeed be quite preposterous and incredulous for a Greenlander to think that his dear country was up for sale. However, one never knows for sure what with America's penchant for creating quagmires and stasis points like Vietnam, Iraq and Afghanistan. Add to that the world's history of Imperialism, Colonialism and the fact that history has been clogged with and chock-full of wars that nobody thought would happen and a pulpit aiming American administration and it becomes clear all things are possible and Greenland could indeed end up as a future flashpoint. But, yes, presently it looks quite improbable and the average Greenlander can be assured of his good night's sleep.

The Benelux Countries

Belgium

The Belgian Prime Minister is Alexander De Croo who is preceded by Sophie Wilmes, Charles Yves Ghislaine Michel(now European Council President), Louis Laurent and many others. The first Belgian King who took charge when Belgium became independent in 1835 was Leopold I. Belgian Interior Ministers include the incumbent Annelies Verlinden preceded by Pieter De Crem, Jan Jambon of the Flemish Party and Anniemie Turtleboom. Other Interior Ministers include the first Jean Frans Tielsman, Isidore Fallon of Katholik Parti, Charles Rogier, Victor Jacob, Henri Jaspar of Katholik Parti and others. Justice Ministers include the incumbent Vincent Van Quickenborne, his predecessor Koeen Geens of the Greens who was preceded by Maggie De Block, Annimie Turtleboom and others.

Netherlands

The Dutch Prime Minister is Mark Rutte, a stickler for squeaky clean, anti-septic cleanliness and who according to Pew Research a couple of years(as of 2021) back topped the popularity charts(his Ace was, perhaps, his penchant for cleanliness in Denmark and other popular issues) in a list of world leaders that included Indonesian President Joko Widodo as the 2nd most popular leader with Prime Minister Modi of India coming up third. However, Modi's popularity fell consequent upon abrogation of Article 370. However, with rumblings being heard that the Modi government is thinking of restoring statehood to Jammu and Kashmir, Modi's popularity may see a spike. Incidentally, as per Pew, former US President Trump in his time was one of the most unpopular leaders in the world with over 70% of the American population disapproving of him which is perhaps why he could not win the reelection. Other Dutch Prime Ministers include former United Nations Commissioner for Refugees Antony Fredriksson "Rudd" Lubbers who was born in Rotterdam and died in Rotterdam on February 14th, 2018.

To the question as to why Netherlands is often called Holland there is a interesting explanation. The term, actually, is a misnomer. North and South Holland are, actually, only two of the several states of Holland. And Soccer fans did not help either. The Dutch King is King Phillipe who along with the Dutch Queen paid a state visit to India in 2015.

Luxemborg

Luxemborg, the world's only sovereign grand Duchy is helmed by the Duke of Luxemborg, currently Henri. And Guillame is the hereditary Grand Duke.

The Prime Minister, currently Xavie Bettel, is the head of Government. Former Prime Ministers include former European Commissioner Jean Claude Juncker and others.

Leichtenstein

Leichtenstein, which shares its Independence Day with India and is one of only two doubly-landlocked countries in the world(the other being Uzbekistan, a doubly-landlocked country being one where one has to cross two borders to reach the border of the country) is helmed by its President, Albert Frick and the Prime Minister is Adrian Hasler while the Vice President is Daniel Risch.

"The Forgotten Republics"

Lithuania

Prime Minister of Lithuania is Ingrida Symonette who is preceded as Premier by Saulius Skervnalis, a member of the Siemas, the Lithuanian Parliament. The President is Gitanas Nauseda. Lithuania's Foreign Minister is Gabriel Bergestens and Lithuania is one among only 13 countries in the world(India not being one of them) to recognise Taiwan and Mr. Bergestens and Taiwan's Foreign Minister Joseph Wu had a tete e tete 2021.

Latvia

The Prime Minister of Latvia is Arthur Kristjanis Karins, a former Minister of the Economy and MEP or Member of European Parliament. The President is Egils Levits.

Estonia

The President of Estonia, the poorest country in the European Union, is Kersti Kaljulaid who is also the Supreme Commander of the Armed Forces of Estonia and the Prime Minister is the recently elected(Feb.2021) Kaja Kallas of the Estonia Reform Party making Estonia the only country in the world to have both a woman

President and a woman Prime Minister. Kaja Kallas's predecessor was Juri Ratas during whose tenure the US Ambassador to Estonia Desmond Melville put in his papers saying then US President Donald Trump was ignoring some of his European allies, esp. the small ones like Estonia.

Cyprus

The Cypriot President is Nicos Anastasiades. Under the Cypriot Constitution, the President has to be Greek and the Vice President has to be a Turkish Cypriot but since 1963 the Turkish Cypriots are not participating in Government

Northern Cyprus

The President of Northern Cyprus, the newest country in the world, is Eric Saner.

Turkey

The founder of modern Turkey, the 28th member of NATO and the EU, where East meets West, is President Mustafa Kemal Ataturk(also the first Speaker of the Grand Assembly, the Turkish Parliament) who founded modern Turkey from the remnants of the Ottoman Empire in 1920. The incumbent President is Recep Tayyip Erdogan(he is also the Speaker of the Grand Assembly) who 2019 assumed sweeping powers including the power to impose the death penalty at will prompting European Parliament President Antonio Tajani to take a swipe at him and come out heavily against his autocratic move. Before the Prime Minister's post was abolished under the 2017 constitutional referendum the last Prime Minister was Binali Yildrim, he is preceded by Ahmet Davutoglu, Abdullah Gul of the Justice and Development Party of Kemal Ataturk, Ismet Inonu, Ali Bozer and others. Abdullah Gul also served a term as Turkish President before Recep Tayyip Erdogan. The Turkish

Foreign Minister is Mevlut Cavusoglu of the Justice and Development Party. Mr.Erdogan has appointed his son-in-law Berat Albayrak as the Finance Minister. The first Foreign Minister was Bekir Sami Kunduh of the Justice and Development Party. The Turkish Vice President is Faut Oktay. Turkey is constructing the Ilisu Dam over the Euphrates and this has set off a water crisis in neighbouring Iraq and Iran prompting India's "Waterman" Magsaysay Award winner Rajendra Singhji to warn a meeting of the Finance Ministers of these countries that the future wars would be 'water wars'. In India's case there is a problem of not too less water but too much water leading to a glut, wastage and other problems. So India which is endowed with abundant water resources should take a leaf out of the experience of these countries and manage its water resources efficiently. Also there was a bad accident at the Soma coal mine in Turkey in which 300 miners were killed.

Albania

Albania's most famous citizen is, of course, Anjeze Gonze Bojaxiu(pronounced as Ansus Gonse Jaxu). Born Aug 26th and the name meaning rose bud, she is better known as Mother Teresa. She later took Indian citizenship and was awarded India's highest honour, the Bharat Ratna in 2010. The Presidents of Albania, a rotating one, are Ilir Meta and Bujar Nishani. The Prime Minister, Edi Rama, is a versatile diplomat, writer, volleyball player, artist and politician all in one. The first President was Ahmet Zogu of the National Socialist Party.

IV
Eastern Europe

The Balkans

Czech Republic

The Czech President is Milos Zeman who 2019 won reelection for a 2nd term and the Prime Minister is Andrej Babis, since 2017,of the ANO 2011 and the 12th person in the office. Preceding him is Bohuslav Sobotka. Pior to becoming Premier, Babis was the country's Finance Minister and former Deputy Prime Minister for the Economy from Jan 2014 to May 2017 when he took over as Premier. Before entering politics, Babis was a successful businessman and entrepreneur.

Slovakia

The President of Slovakia, the second poorest country in the European Union after Estonia with Greece saying that rich European countries like Greece could not bankroll and bailout poor European countries like Slovakia if the latter do not buckle up and run a tight ship, is Zuzana Caputova who is preceded by Andrej

Kiska. Prime Minister Igor Matovic recently(2021) swapped roles with Finance Minister Eduard Heger on the orders of President Zuzana Caputova. Matovic's predecessor was Peter Pellegrini who succeeded Robert Fico who was given the boot following the murder of a prominent journalist, a murder following which the head of Interior Minister Robert Kalinak also rolled. As the Germans say *Kopfs Wurfeln* or prominent heads rolled after the murder. Mr.Pellegrini held many prominent positions before helming the country including the post of Deputy Prime Minister for Investments and Information.

Serbia

The Serb President is Alexander Vucic and the Prime Minister is Ana Branbic who is the openly gay Prime Minister in the world. She was preceded in the Prime Minister's post by Felipe Plenkovic. Then, there were, of course, the butcher pair of Serbia-Bosnia Herzogovnia, President Slobodan Milosevic and his notorious General Ratko Mladic, both of were sent to prison by the Hague based International Court of Justice for genocide, the court to try war criminals. Incidentally, Fatou Bensouda became the first African to sit on the Court and India's Dalveer Bhandari(who pipped an English Judge to the post) could queer the pitch for Pakistan in case of the Indian prisoner on death row(sentenced to death for espionage)in Pakistan, Kulbhushan Jadhav although the honorable Justices are supposed to be fully neutral. As is well known, the Dayton Accords of the 1,990s settled the Serbian conflict with Serbia and Bosnia Herzogovnia becoming two separate republics.

Bosnia Herzogovnia

The President of Bosnia Herzogovnia is Mladen Ivanic and Dennis Zvizdic is the Prime Minister. A former Deputy Prime Minister was Hakija Turajlic who was killed in 1,993.

Croatia

The Croatian President is Zoran Milanovic who is preceded at the helm by Milorad Dodik, Kolinda Grabar Kitarovic who was the star at the FIFA World Cup a few years back(as of 2021) in Russia egging on and spiritedly supporting her country's team which put up a sterling show as they went down with their guns blazing against defenders France and others. The Prime Minister is Andrej Plenkovic. Croatia has a provision for several Deputy Prime Ministers, the Deputy Prime Minister being appointed by the President and usually holding one important portfolio like Finance or Home and serving at the pleasure of the Cabinet and has to resign if the opposition passes a motion of no-confidence against him or her. The incumbent Deputy Prime Ministers are Tomo Medved(sworn in July 23rd, 2020), Davor Bozinovic(sworn in July 19th, 2020), Dravko Maric(sworn in July 19th, 2020) and Boris Milosevic(sworn in July 23rd, 2020). The first Deputy Prime Ministers were Mate Babic and others.

Slovenia

The President of Slovenia is Lojge Peterle and his predecessor was Borut Pahor. The President is a member of the General Affairs Council, Strategic Affairs Council, National Security Council and the Cabinet. The Prime Minister is Janez Jansa who was preceded by Marjan Sarec who in turn was preceded by one-time Foreign Minister, MP, Chairman of the National Assembly, lawyer, Prof. of Law, University of Lubljana, Faculty of Law Miroslav 'Miro' Cerar, an outsider to politics whose pedecessor was Alenqa Bratusek and others. Some of them like Janez Jansa Alenqa Bratusek served multiple terms. The Foreign Minister is a member of the Foreign Affairs Council, Strategic Affairs Council, National Security Council and the Cabinet. Foreign Ministers include the incumbent Anze Logar, his predecessor Miroslav 'Miro' Cerar, Zoran Thaler, Lojge Peterle, the first Foreign Minister Dmitrij Rupel who paid two visits to India, during the first visit in 2006 he requested for Slovenia's membership in the Non-Aligned Movement and Foreign Minister Anand Sharma acceded to the request. He was back in 2010, this time to attend a Art of Living session in Bangalore but he did not go back before meeting senior Indian government officials in Delhi and others.

Moldova

The Moldovan President is Maia Sandu who is into her second term and the Prime Minister is former Finance Minister Natalia Gavrilita who is also into her second term as Prime Minister with Marie Aureliu preceding her as Acting Prime Minister and other Prime Ministers include Giorgi Gakharia, Mamuka Bhaktanadze, Pavel Filip, a one time Finance Minister who was Finance Minister in former President Ion Chicu's Cabinet and others. President Ion Chicu in whose Cabinet Maia Sandu was Finance Minister was preceded as President by Maia Sandu but it was a short honeymoon for Miss Sandu as she soon had to make way for Ion Chicu who was Finance Minister in Sandu I Cabinet. Before Sandu I it was Igor Dodon who was President. Incidentally, the currency of Moldova is the Leu which like the Rumanian Leu is divisible into 100 Bani, 50 Bani, 20 Bani, 10 Bani etc. That is, it is divisible by a power of 10.

North Macedonia

The North Macedonian Prime Minister, a country whose name 2019 was changed from Macedonia to North Macedonia in a referendum, Oliver Spaskovski and President Stevo Pendarovski 2021 swapped roles. President Stevo Pendarovski was preceded as President by George Ivanov under whom the Prime Minister was Zoran Zaev, an economist who previously served as Mayor of Strumica. The first President of North Macedonia, way back in 1,990, was at the time was the oldest leader in the world.

Georgia

The incumbent Prime Minister of Georgia is Iraqli Garibashvili, preceded by Bedzina Ivanishvili preceded by Kvrikashvili whose President was the academic and politician Giorgi Margvilasvili who was the fourth President of Georgia. The first President of Georgia was the former Soviet Foreign Minister Eduard Shevadnadze who was followed in the hotseat by Zvaid Ghamsakhurdia who holds a Doctorate in Philosophy, Mikhail Shakashvili, Vladimir Ivanov and the present President Salome Zourabichvili.

Montenegro

The Prime Minister of Montenegro, who was slighted by former US President Donald Trump once again highlighting the slipshod treatment meted out by Mr.Trump to some of his smaller European allies(remember what US Ambassador to Estonia said), is Dusko Markovic. Whatever there were a lot of ruffled feathers in Montenegro after the incident. The President of Montenegro is Felipe Juvajovnic. Montenegro until recently boasted of the tallest pier in the world, a whopping 139m. However, Manipur's Jiribaum-Imphal-Tupul line project is now the tallest pier in the world with a height of 143m. Montenegro is also home to some of the finest bridges in the world like the Duerdinica bridge.

Kosovo

Kosova 2021 got a new President, its second female leader, former Parliament Speaker Vjosa Osmani Sadriu who is preceded by a long retinue of Presidents. The Prime Ministers include the incumbent Albin Kurti into his second term, his predecessor, Avatullah Hoti, Ramush Haradinaj, Hashim Thaci, Bajram Rexhefi, Bajram Kosumi, Imer Pula, Ali Shukriu, the first Prime Minister, Fadil Hoxa and others.

Romania

The Prime Minister of Rumania is Klaus Iahoniss and the President is Mihai Tudose.

Bulgaria

The President of Bulgaria is Rumen Radev who is also the Supreme Commander of the Armed Forces of Bulgaria. His deputy is the Prime Minister Boyko Metodiev Borrisov. Bulgaria's 1st Vice President is Illiana Mafinova Ivatova and the 2nd Vice President is Margarita Poparova. Boyko Borrisov is a former Mayor of Sofia.(2005-2009). The Presidential Palace is Boyana Palace, Sofia. The first President of Bulgaria was Zhelyn Zhalev who won the 1,992 Presidential election by direct popular vote under the new Constitution and is a Doctor in Philosophy. His Vice President was Blaga Dmitrinov and the second President was Peter Stoyanov who won the 1,996 election and helmed the country.

Ukraine

This country at the ramparts of Central Europe is strategically placed between East and West which is why it suffered a split with Russia annexing Crimea, much to the consternation of the West. Now again Russia's ever territory thirsty President Vladimir Putin plans to invade Ukraine in what is steady attrition of Ukranian territory as part of Mr. Putin's pan East European "occupation vision" though Jan 2022 he claimed he was undecided. This has not stopped the America led West from pressing the alarm button and upping its ante with countries like America and Britain even undertaking recon missions and the British have even supplied weapons like anti tank missiles etc. to Ukraine circumnavigating around a reluctant Germany which has flatly refused to supply arms to Ukraine. The Russian Foreign Minister Sergei Victorovich Lavrov has also held talks with Ukraine's Foreign Minister Dmitro

Kuleba even as Putin amasses troops on the Ukrainian border and a Russian invasion of Ukraine does indeed look imminent. This writer has dealt with the Russian invasion of Ukraine in depth in his book World Military Order. The President of Ukraine is Vlodymyr Zelensky and the First Lady is Olena Zelensky. While the Prime Minister is Shmyhal Denya, Stefan Kubiv is the 1st Deputy Prime Minister with senior civil servant Olha Vitalyivna Stefanishyna taking over as Deputy Prime Minister for European and Euro-Atlantic integration. The Deputy Prime Minister for Re-integration of Temporarily Occupied Territories is Oleksii Remnikov with whom EU Secretary General discussed the security situation in and around Ukraine and the EU's political and practical support to Kyiv. The Minister for Economic Development and Trade is Oleksy Llubchenko. The incumbent President Vlodymyr Zelensky's predecessor was Petro Poroshenko. A former President was the Russian-leaning Viktor Yanukovich who after he was deposed was said to be suffering from Schizoprenia in Moscow. A former Prime Minister was Yulia Tymoshenko and Oleksander Turchynov was a Interim Speaker who presided over the interim sessions of Ukraine's Parliament before change of administrations at the helm.

Hungary

The President of Hungary is Victor Orban whom former Vice President Hamid Ansari met in Budapest in a sign of expanding bilateral cooperation. The Prime Minister of Hungary is Janos Ader.

Malta

PMs of Malta include Dominic "Dom" Mintoff(born August 6th), Jack Howard, John Howard, the incumbent Roger Abela and others. Presidents include John Howard, Jack Howard, the incumbent George Abela and others.

Home and Foreign Ministers include Carmelo Abela who held both portfolios including being Minister of International Trade, MP and currently he heads the Labor Party. Political parties include Labour Party, Agrarian League, the Liberals and others.

Then, there is, of course, the small Kingdom of Monaco which is the oldest country in Europe.

V
South East Asia

Thailand

In 1922 King Prajadhipok of Thailand gave the people of Siam their first Constitution. Under the Constitution the Prime Minister although appointed by the King serves at the pleasure of Parliament and has to resign if the latter passes a motion of no confidence against him or her although this has never happened in practice. The present Thai King is Maha Vajiralonkorn or Rama X of the Chakri dynasty. Vajiralonkorn who recently married ascended the throne following the death of the previous King Tinsulanonda Bhumibol Adulyadej who in his time was the oldest monarch in the world. Currently, at 92, Queen Elizabeth II of England is the oldest monarch in the world. The various Thai Prime Ministers include the incumbent Gen. Prayut Chan O Cha, Myetin Shinawatra, Abhijit Widjayajiva, Somchai Wongsawat, Myetin Shinawatra's father Thakshin Shinawatra,Samak Sundaravej, Surayud Chulanont, Chuan Leekpai, Supachai Panichpakdi, Pote Sarasin, Sarit Thanarat, Seni Pramoj, Kukrit Pramoj, Anand Panrayachun, Sanya Dharmashakti, Prem Tinsulanonda, Acting Prime Minister Niwatamrong Boomsangpaisan and a long retinue of distinguished Prime Ministers. The Agriculture Minister is Grisada Boonrach who was sent as the Thai Prime Minister's Special Envoy to Prime Minister Modi's swearing-in ceremony during the latter's second term.

Philippines

Philippines which alongwith countries such as India, Columbia and Bulgaria got a rating upgrade from BBB to -BB(and these countries are now economically ahead of even advanced countries like Italy which was rated at BBB) has been led by Presidents such as Emilio Eguinaldo Y Famy de Y Famy, who was the first and in his time the youngest President of Asia, the legendry Ramon Magsaysay who was at the helm from 1954-59 and after whom the Ramon Magsaysay Award was instituted which until the advent of the Gandhi Peace Prize was known as the Nobel Prize of Asia, another legendary President Ferdinand De Marcos, his spouse and 'Iron Butterfly' Imelda Marcos, Prof.Gloria Maria Macaraeg de Macapagal Arroyo, the actor film star and 9th Vice President Jose Macapagal de Macapagal, Speaker Sergio Suico Osmena who died in Quezon City, Corazan Aquino, Manuel Baxter the incumbent Rodrigo Duterte who is seen as anti-American but that didn't prevent Washington from making a peace overture to Beijing routed through Manila although Beijing and Manila have disputes over what China calls the 9 dot line and what Phillipines calls the 11 dot line and by which they are separated and others.

Beijing and Manila also differ over the status of the Spratly Islands, Maclasfield Bank, Pratas and other strategically located islands in the South China Sea through which 2/3rds of the world's oil, some 3 billion barrels a day, flows alongwith the Straits of Hormuz. China also has an ongoing dispute with Vietnam(which it invaded) over Pratas. Indeed cussed and quarrelsome China cannot seem to get alongwith half a dozen of its neighbours in the South China Sea. As PM Modi said "China reveals a primitive 18th century mindset not respecting national sovereignty or international territorial waters". Some of the world's oldest and quaint aborigines and tribes are found in these contested islands.

The 14th and current Vice President is lawyer and social activist Leni Maria Obrador while senators include lawyer, and activist Prof.Leila de Lima and Tito Sutto is the Senate President who under the Constitution of Philippines takes over as the President in case of temporary leave, absence, resignation or dismissal of the President. Speakers include the first Sergio Suico Osmena who died in Quezon City, Alvaro Cayo Teodoro Locsin, one Speaker belonging to the LDP and others. Dy.Speakers include Paulo Rodrigue Duterte who studied at the Phillipines Women's University and others.

Singapore

The first President of Singapore was Yusof Ishak(prior office-first Malayan-born Yang di Pertuan Negara) who took charge after the country's independence from Great Britain on August 9th, 1965, who was followed by Benjamin Sheares(a former Medical Practioner), Devan Nair(prior office-MP for Anston), Ong Teng Cheong(prior office-Deputy Prime Minister), Wee Kim Wee(prior office-Ambassador to South Korea), Wee Kim Wee was the first to use custodial powers when he used it in 1993, S.R.Nathan(prior office-Ambassador-at-Large), S.R. Nathan was the longest serving President serving from 1999 to 2011, Ng Eng Hen(prior office-Defense Minister), Tony Tan Keng Yam(prior office-Deputy Prime Minister) and the incumbent Halimah Youcob(first woman and second Malay-born President, prior office-Speaker of Parliament). Halimah Youcob became President under a provision of Singapore's Constitution under which it is mandatory to elect a Malay-born as President thorough a reserved election if the same has not been done for the past three election cycles. And also the terms of these Presidents were periodically interspersed with Acting Presidents some of whom were Supreme Court Chief Justices, Speakers of Parliament and the senior civil servant Javier Yubraj Manuel Pillai who served as Acting President on as many as 65 occassions spread across discontinuos stints when the President was away abroad be it to Africa, Europe and other places and who has been conferred Singapore's highest honor Order of Nila Utama or First Citizen Award and has been described as "best brain" by Singapore's first Prime Minister Lee Kuan Yew and who was born to a Malay-origin Christian father and Jaffna-born Sri Lankan mother and others. Singapore till date has had only three Prime Ministers the first Lee Kuan Yew who was a admirer of India and Nehru for its adherence to democratic principles and values, Goh Chok Tung and the incumbent Lee Hsein Loong who is the eldest son of the first Prime Minister Lee Kuan Yew and also Chairman of ASEAN. Singapore's Finance Minister is Heng Swee Keat and the Foreign Minister is Vivian Balakrishnan.

Malaysia

The Malaysian Prime Minister is Muhyuddin Yassin who succeeded Mahamatir Mohammed who at 93 was then the oldest leader in the world who in turn succeeded Najib Tun Razak. Incidentally, Najib Tun Razak was embroiled in the Panama papers scandal which took the heads of other bigwigs like former Pakistani Prime Minister Nawaz Sharif, his daughter Maryum, former Iceland President Bjarni Benedictsson and others.During his tenure as Prime Minister Mahatir Mohammed released his protege Anwar Ibrahim who is a prospective future Prime Minister.

Ministry of Foreign Affairs(Kemeterian Luar Negeri)

The Ministry of Foreign Affairs also known as Wisma Putra which is also the name of its building in Putrajaya is responsible for foreign affairs, diaspora affairs, foreign relations, bilateral affairs, multilateral affairs, ASEAN etc is headed by the Foreign Minister.

Saifudin Abdullah and Kamarudin Jaffar are the two Foreign Ministers. Raja Nusrul Zainil Abidin is the Deputy Minister for Foreign Affairs while Rahimi Harun is the Secretary General(Management Services). Dato Sri Hishamudin Tun Hussien was the Foreign Minister before the incumbents and Ramlan Ibrahim was the Secretary General(Bilateral Affairs)

Ministry of Health(Kemeterian Kesihatan)

The Ministry of Health or Kemeterian Kesihatan in Malay is responsible for public health system, universal health care, immunization programs, leprosy control, dental care and the like.

Khairy Jamaludin is the Health Minister and Aaron Ago Dagong is the Deputy Minister for Health. While Leong Yew Koh was the first Health Minister, Dr. Adham Baba was the Health Minister immediately before the incumbent.

Ministry of Finance(Kemeterian Kewangan)

The Ministry of Finance is charged with government expenditure and revenue raising. A key duty of the Finance Minister is the presentation of the Federal Budget in the month of October every year.

The Malaysian Minister of Finance is Tekgku Zafrul Tengku Abdul Aziz and Mohammed Shahar Abdullah is the Deputy Minister of Finance while Henry Lee Hau Suk is the very first Minister of Finance. Asri Bin Hamidon is the Secretary General(Treasury) and Deputy Secretary General(Treasury), Othman Bin Semail is the Deputy Secretary General(Investment) while Zakaiah Binti Zafar is also the Deputy Secretary General(Investment).

Indonesia

Indonesia till date has had 7 Presidents. On August 17,1945 Indonesia declared its independence from the Dutch but it was not until 2005 that the Dutch recognized that date as the official date for Indonesia's independence. In 1945 the occupying Japanese Army formed the Preparatory Committee for Indonesia's Independence and Sukarno became the first President of Indonesia followed by Suharto, Bachruddin Jusuf Habibie B.J.Habibie, Abdulrahim Waheed, Megawati Sukarnoputri, Susilo Bambangang Yudhoyono and the present President Joko Widodo. The Presidential Jet is Air Indonesia 1 and the Indonesian President is decorated with as many as 14 decorations chief among which is the San Bantan. Indonesia is the world's third most populous Muslim nation after Saudi Arabia and India respectively. The Indonesian Vice President is Jusuf Kella and he shared the office until recently(2020) with Marouf Amin. Marouf Amin has since resigned. Marouf Amin was originally in the PKDP, then he changed parties to PDP and now he is an Independent. This shows that political humpty dumpties and fence sitters are not the bane of India alone and they extend all the way from America to Australia to Indonesia. The Indonesian Foreign Minister is Retno Marsudi while the Vice Minister for Foreign Affairs is Mahendra Siregar and the Health Minister is Budi Gunadi Sidikin.

Myanmar

Myanmar's President is Mint Swe who was preceded by Wynn Mint. The Prime Ministers include the incumbent, Min Aung LWin, former Prime Minister Thein Sein, Soe Win, the first Prime Minister U Nu and others. The State Counsellors(a post akin to Prime Minister) include Nobel Laureate Aung Sang Syu Kyi who came to power through a by-election and is a former Foreign Minister and others. Aung Sang Syu Kyi alongwith former President, Wynn Mint has since been jailed by the new military junta headed by President Mint Swe which came to power after the 2021 coup de et. Other Foreign Ministers include Wunna Muang Lwin and others. Until recently, everyone from experts to astrologers were agreed that Myanmar's future was dull. But, not anymore. With the ushering in of democracy things have changed for the better. But, with the 2021 coup de et, doubts again seem to have been cast on Myanmar's future. Myanmar, a chequered democracy to spice up the claim to democracy at best, seems to perennially swing between largely military ruled juntas and democracy. Myanmar's festering wound is the Rohingya problem in Myanmar's Rakhane Valley. The homeless Rohingya refugees are causing problems for nations around the world from India to Bangladesh. Also Aung Sang Syu Kyi's popularity nosedived on account of her tough approach to the Rohingya crisis.

Vietnam

Vietnam 2021 elected a new President, former Prime Minister Nguyen Xuan Phuc whose predecessor was Nguyen Phu Trong whose prior office was General Secretary of the Communist Party of Vietnam(CPV) which is a real power center in Vietnam. He continues to be the General Secretary of the CPV. Prior to him the President was Tran Dai Quang who died in office consequent upon which Nguyen Phu Trong became President. The Prime Minister is Pham Minh Chinh who was preceded by Nguyen Xuan Phuc while the Vice President is Vo Thi Anh Xuan and the Defense Minister is Army General Phan Van Giang who is preceded by Ngo Xuan Lich. The Information and Broadcasting Minister is Nguyen Manh Hung. The Cam Rahn naval base in Vietnam was the largest Soviet naval base outside of the Western Hemisphere during the time of the Cold War. On the topic of the Cold War, it is worth noting that in the context of big power politics during the Cold War, actually countries like Vietnam and Egypt to some extent and major countries like India and China escaped all orbits and emerged as independent orbits in themselves. For e.g. Anwar Sadat of Egypt took a sharp 180 degrees turn and broke bread with and signed a peace treaty with Israel's Menachem Begin under the aegis of the Camp David talks sponsored by Washington. He veered Egypt clear of all Arab instrasigence with the attendant talk of "driving the Jews into the sea". He paid with his life when he was gunned down as he was stepping out of his personal jet on the tarmac of Cairo airport. Arab fundamentalists("that coward Sadat" to them) were suspected to be behind the assassination. For the courageous move, Sadat along with Begin and Yasser Arafat was conferred the 1994 Peace Nobel.

Former Indian Ambassador to Vietnam Preeti Saran whose husband Pankaj Saran is a former Indian Ambassador to Russia presented her credentials to 6th President of Vietnam Trang Tan Sang and incumbent President Nguyen Phu Trong paid a State visit to India in 2020 and paid tribute to Rajiv Gandhi. India and Vietnam also held military exercises in 2020 in a sign of expanding bilateral military cooperation. Ho Chi Minh was the first President of Vietnam and the first General Secretary of the Communist Party of Vietnam(CPV). A senior American official on a State Visit to Vietnam touched off a raw nerve when he said the wrong side had won the Vietnam War, an allegory to Vietnam's economic backwardness. Many Americans opine that the Vietnam War resulted in the phenomenon called Donald Trump that went by.

Cambodia

Cambodia's PM is Hun Sen and the King is Norodom Sihamoni, son of former King, the legendary Norodom Sihanouk who abdicated the throne in favour of his son in 2004. Vice Presidents include Chea Sim and others. However, PM Hun Sen wants his 44 year old son Hun Manet to contest the polls on his party Cambodia Peoples Party ticket and succeed him. And Chea Sim and others have since given way to Men Kam Yan, Ke Kim Yan, Prak Sokhonn and Aun Pommoniroth all of the ruling Cambodia Peoples Party. China is assidously wooing Cambodia. For e.g. 2020 it acquired the Ream naval base in Cambodia, its first in South East Asia on a 99-year lease in a region which China considers an extension of its territory on the Pacific seaboard based on Hainan island where China's secret submarine base is located. Also, the region is crucial to China's controversial Belt and Road Initiative(BRI) spanning four continents, Asia, Africa, Europe and Australia and extending over 60,000 km, an Initiative which has rankled the nerves of countries like India and Germany but applied balm on the nerves of countries like Morroco, Angola and others. The base can house troops, berth warships and has other modern facilities. India too should find an answer to Ream and in this context Indian Ambassador to Cambodia, Devyani Khobragade has a job on her hands. This is crucial if India is to accept the gauntlet and take on the Dragon in South East Asia, a region which is increasingly emerging as a theatre of Superpower rivalry led by the United States and China.

The new Chinese Ambassador to the United States Qin Gang, a former Vice Minister of Foreign Affairs, has little American experience unlike his predecessor, Cui Tiankai, a graduate of Normal University of Peking, who is an old America hand. In view of the increasing importance of the position let's list out the different Chinese Ambassadors to the United States. They are as follows: Alfred Sao Zu See, Zhou Shukai, Shen Jianlong and others during the time of the China Republic. After the establishment of diplomatic relations between the United States and the People's Republic of China in May 1975 soon after the UN recognized China, the first Chinese Ambassador to the United States was Huang Zhen, also the first Chinese Ambassador to Hungary who was followed by Chai Zemin, Zhang Wenjin, Zhu Qizhen, Han Xu, Li Daoyu, Li Zhaoxing, later a Foreign Minister of China, Yang Jiechi also a Foreign Minister who is now one of the State Counsellors, Zhou Wenzhong, Zhang Yesui, Cui Tiankai and the incumbent Qin Gang.

Concurrently, the first American Commissioner to China as American diplomatic representatives to China were then known was former Associate Justice(Judge of the United States Supreme Court) William Celeb Cushing who as Commissioner signed the Treaty of Wanghia in 1844. From 1844 to 1857 Commissioners represented the United States in China. Until 1898 the Qing Empire did not have a system in place to accept Letters of Credence from foreign representatives. From 1854 to 1935 America's chief diplomatic representative in China was known as Minister Plenipotentiary. In 1935 the Mission in Nanking was upgraded to that of an Embassy and the position of Minister Plenipotentiary was upgraded to the higher rank of Ambassador and Leonard

Woodcock was appointed as the first United States Ambassador to China who was followed by Arthur. W. Hummel Jr., Winston Lord and a long glitterati of Ambassadors like former Utah Lt. Governor Jon Huntsman Jr. who was later appointed US Ambassador to Russia, the longest serving Iowa Governor(total 22 years) Terry Branstead, Gary Locke, Robert. W. Forden, David Meale the incumbent R. Nicholas Burns, a former US Ambassador to Greece and others.

Taiwan

Taiwan's President is Ms. Tsai-Ing Wen. The President of the Executive Yuan is Chen Jian while the President of the Legislative Yuan is Su-Jia Chuan.

Health Ministry

Taiwan's Ministry of Health is responsible for aspects of health like universal immunization programmes, cancer, cancer research and the like.

The Health Minister is Chen Won Chung with the Deputy Minister of Health portfolio going to Hseue Jui-Yuan. Chen Chaw Min is a former Secretary General, Ministry of Health.

Laos

The President of Laos People's Democratic Republic is Bounhang Vorachit who ranks fourth in Laos's Communist Party Politburo. The Prime Minister is Thongloun Sisolouth who was educated at the Gennady Stenusteny Institute in Russia and President Vorachit 2018 accepted the credentials of Bahraini Ambassador to Laos Ahmed Abdullah Al Hajeri.

Brunei

The Sultan of the oil rich Sultanate of Brunei is Hassanal Bolkaiah who is one of the richest men in the world.

VI
South Asia

India

Apart from the Indian Prime Ministers[Incidentally, Prime Minister Narendra Modi Jan 2022 opened an entirely new front in the global war against terror. He talked of a concerted, continued and sustained global campaign to malign and run down India and protray India as "lynchyistan". India's Ambassador to the UN T.S.Trimurti too dwelt with it at length at and junior mission staff like First Secretary Sneha Dubey are sure to follow up on the Prime Minister and the Ambassador's statements. Elaborating, the Prime Minister said this new war against India is undertaken principally by China's PLA but also involves its bellweather and all weather ally Pakistan. According to him this is a package that comes in three parts:Psychological Warfare, Media Warfare and Legal Warfare. And Psychological Warfare overlaps into Media Warfare. In this kind of warfare, the center of gravity of the war shifts from the Army of the country to the people of the country. While needless to say the respective militaries of the countries continue to stay engaged, a new front is opened up by our enemies(read China and Pakistan in that order)-the people of the country. Dwelling on the topic at length, the Prime Minister offered specific examples to buttress his arguments:the Haridwar incident where a Muslim cleric talked of "Hindu genocide" and called for "changing the map of India"(in his words "Hindustan ka Naksha badal dalenge" terrifying comments indeed), a Durga Puja Temple pandal was attacked, an ISKCON priest was killed, and Hindu deities were destroyed(also "the Christianity in threat" bogey is being raised by our enemies and as part of this narrative, we can offer the the case of The Sisters of Charity FCRA row. BJP ideologue Ram Madhav said while the government had cancelled the licenses of as many as 100 NGOs, an attempt was made by select sections to highlight the Sisters of Charity case. Mr. Madhav called this politics of victimhood), even externally a Hindu temple was attacked in Pakistan and in general a fear psychosis, Hindu phobia, and Hate India campaign has been unleashed. Calling on the people of the country to rise above petty partisan politics, the Prime Minister said this was the time for unity, not petty politics, not the time for a slugfest between the Lutyens ecosystem and the right wing ecosystem, an ecosystem which has incresingly been hijacked by Mr.Modi as a "Modi tsunami" is unleashed in the country, as a Modi "wave" takes over the country and Mr.Modi used Parliament as a platform to voice his misgivings about the Congress and used it to apply atmospheric pressure, ecosystemic pressure on the Congress and interestingly he singled out the Congress as he sought to drive a wedge between the Congress and the rest of the opposition. Mr.Modi also said post-World War II, a new world order had taken shape in which we are all living in today, but, post-Covid-19 a new world order is taking shape and India should keep its trsyst with destiny and leave its indelible footprint on the world. And as if to bear out the PM's words, the country posted a healthy growth rate of 9% as per Central government figures. The World Bank also said India is likely to keep its date with growth fiscal 2020-21](Atal Behari Vajpayee, the gentle colossus who strode over the Indian political canvass like a colossus for decades and soared high above the sins and transgressions of his party was the only non-Congress Prime Minister to complete his term in office) and Presidents who are well known to most Indians, the first Vice-President to succeed his immediate superior was Sarvepalli Radhakrishnan, the second Vice President who served discontinuos stints as Vice-Chancellor of Mysore University, Vice-Chancellor of Andhra University, Ambassador to the U.S.S.R., Vice-President and finally President, the first Vice-President not to succeed his immediate superior was Gopal Swarup Phatak, other Vice-Presidents who did not succeed their immediate superior are Bassappa Danappa Jatti, B.D. Jatti, former Chief Minister of Karnataka, Governor of Orissa and Lt. Governor of Pondicherry, Mohammed Hidayatullah, Rajasthan ka ek hi Singh former Rajasthan Chief Minister Bhairon Singh Shekhawat, Krishna Kant and whether the incumbent Mupavarapu Venkaiah Naidu of Nellore, Andhra Pradesh succeeds in becoming President remains to be seen. President Ramnath Kovind who represented U.P. in the Rajya Sabha from 1994 to 2006 is the first person from U.P. to become President. This writer will deal with the Indian Political System in depth in a different book. Suffice it to say that R.K. Shamukham Chetty was the first Finance Minister of India(during the Nehruvian era) while Baldev Singh was the first Defence Minister and needless to say Sardar Vallabhbhai Patel who first talked of the steel frame(a reference to the Civil Service) at Metcalfe House while addressing the first batch of Civil Service officers in 1947 was the first Home Minister of India while Nehru was his own Foreign Minister throughout the 17 years of his rule.

Other early Defense Ministers include Vengalil Krishnan Krishna Menon, V.K.Krishna Menon(during the Himalaya War between India and China)(who according to many observers was the second most powerful man in Nehru's Cabinet next only to Nehru) who also served a stint as India's first Ambassador to the United Kingdom, a man whom Britain relentlessly pilliored calling him a "commie" and a "womanizer", Nehru's evil genius. Indeed he was Nehru's astute genius who saved the day for India at the UN on Kashmir. He waxed forth to and fro on Kashmir in a marathon 7 hours 48 minutes speech, collapsed midway, had to be hospitalized but came back, took his seat and insisted on finishing his speech, a speech which has gone down in the annals of the UN as the longest speech by a visiting foreign dignitary. He argued so eloquently that the UN had to support India on Kashmir and the speech also allowed Nehru to gain a temporary foothold on the disputed part of Kashmir, the only time in history India ever did so. However, the speech also gained for Menon a fearsome reputation as a great orator and after the speech American mothers would put their children to sleep saying "if you don't sleep, I will call Krishna Menon"! Other Defense Ministers include Swaran Singh who was also Foreign Minister, Y.B.Chavan during the 1965 Indo-Pak War who was also Maharashtra Chief Minister, Krishna Chandra Pant, K.C.Pant(born 10 August, 1931, Bhowali, United Provinces, British India-died 15th November 2012(aged 81), Delhi, who was the Prime Minister's interlocuter on Kashmir for 26 years, held high constitutional posts including as Civil Aviation Minister, Scientific and Technology Minister, Tourism Minister and held many other cabinet positions in a career spanning 37 years and in more recent times Pranab Mukherjee, A.K.Antony, former Goa Chief Minister Manohar Parikker, Nirmala Sitharaman, the incumbent Rajnath Singh and others. Incidentally, Deputy Prime Ministers include former Haryana Chief Minister Devi Lal, L.K.Advani, former Home Minister and Andhra Pradesh Governor Sushil Kumar Shinde and others. Home Ministers include S.B.Chavan, S.R.Bommai, a former Karnataka Chief Minister whose son Basavaraj Bommai is the incumbent Chief Minister of Karnataka, P.V.Narasimha Rao, Rajnath Singh, the incumbent Amit Shah who some time back sent out instructions to police stations across the country that the day of third-degree methods was past and others.

Foreign Ministers include the incumbent Subhramanyam Jai Shankar, S.JaiShankar, a former Foreign Secretary and Ambassador to the United States and China apart from other countries, his predecessor Sushma Swaraj, S.M.Krishna, Salman Kurshid, P.V.Narasimha Rao, Swaran Singh, Ministers of State for Foreign Affairs Anand Sharma, Thiruvananthapuram M.P. Shashi Tharoor, Gen.(retd.) V.K. Singh who held the additional portfolio of North-

Eastern Affairs, former Janata Dal(S) Vice-President P.Murlidhar, M.J.Akbar, E.Ahamed and others. Finance Ministers include the incumbent the articulate Nirmala Sitharaman, her predecessor the late Arun Jaitley who too was articulate and kicked off his political career by leading the first student protest during the heydays of the Emergency which the British termed was "a blot on their copy book", Pranab Mukherjee, the Harvard educated P. Chidambaram, the Oxford and Cambridge educated former RBI Governor Manmohan Singh who in consonance with Prime Minister Narasimha Rao unleashed a set of economic reforms in the early ninetees that had far-reaching effects and changed the economic landscape and face of the country forever. Paradoxically, the same Manmohan Singh as Prime Minister opted to be a silent spectator as the dual power center obtaining at the Centre due to Sonia Gandhi wreacked havoc across the economic canvas of the country and reversed some of the initial gains. Thankfully, under Prime Minister Modi the country got an upgrade from well known ratings agencies like Moody's proving that the initial economic successes were no flash in the pan. And in her 2022 Budget speech, Finance Minister Nirmala Sitaraman said the country recorded a healthy growth rate of 9.2 % in year ended 2021-22. Ironically, this was higher than the usual growth rate recorded in "non-Covid-19 years". This is inspite of the Covid-19 juggernaut which has sent millions spiralling into the poverty trap. The country is, however, yet to see the double digit growth rates that China has recorded for the past several years if it is to become the next China. Still, our macro economic fundamentals are strong with a rock solid committment to fighting inflation and our meduim term firewalls are solid too, with a comfortable and healthy reserve position. And, currently (as of October 2021) the country is facing a severe coal shortage although the Centre has made it clear coal-fired power plants were in no danger of being shut down. And Manmohan Singh as of October 2021 is suffering from ill health and is admitted in AIIMS. Other Finance Ministers include the Raja of Manda, former Uttar Pradesh Chief Minister Vishwanath Pratap Singh, V.P.Singh who let out a fusillade of protests, a volley of protests across the country by bringing out the Mandal Commission Report from cold storage as his "salvo", a report regarding which Rajiv Gandhi said "its a can of worms, I won't touch it". And, of course, Mr. Singh could not bell the cat that he let out of the bag and cull it. As regards some of the other Finance Ministers there was the stickler for simplicity Madhu Dandavate who made it a point to wash his own clothes during "the Hindu rate of growth" days. Thankfully, those days are long dead and gone as the country has long since come out of the economic doldrums and is now powering itself on the path to economic resurgence and recovery. Apart from the first Finance Minister R.K.Shanmukham Chetty as noted earlier there was also the RBI Governor I.G.Patel who served as Finance Minister from 1955-57. The first Food and Agriculture Minister was former President Babu Rajendra Prasad who also served a stint as AICC President. The first Information and Broadcasting Minister was the first woman Cabinet Minister of India Rajkumari Amrit Kaur. The title of the doctoral thesis that the first Law and Justice Minister B.R.Ambedkar submitted to Columbia University was National Dividend of India and the title of the doctoral thesis that he submitted to London School of Economics was The Problem of the Rupee: its Origins and Sources. Dr. B.R.Ambedkar was of course a highly qaulified man with two Doctorates to his credit, one from Columbia University and the other from the London School of Economics. The first Education Minister of India was Maulana Abul Kalam Azad who too served as INC President. The first Deputy Defense Minister was Majithia.

Among the junior Ministers in the current Cabinet(after the 2021 Cabinet reshuffle) are Railways, Communications, Electronics and IT Minister Ashwini Vaishnav who is a former I.A.S Officer who went to Pennsylvania State University, United States and MBT Engineering College. His junior Minister is Darshana Vikram Jardosh, Minister of State for Railways and Textiles. She is married to Vikram Jardosh. She has been Surat M.P. since 2009 in the 14th, 15th, and the present 17th Lok Sabha. The Education, Skill

Development and Entrepreneurship Minister is former Petroleum and Natural Gas Minister Dharmendra Pradhan while Narayan Tatu Rane is the Micro, Small and Medium Enterprises Minister. While Virendra Singh is the Law and Justice Minister, Sarbanananda Sonowal is the Minister for Social Justice and Empowerment, Pasupati Kumar Paras is the Food Processing Industries Minister being appointed in the place of Harsimrat Kaur Badal. After the death of former Food, Consumer Affairs and Public Distribution Minister Ram Vilas Paswan due to Covid-19, Piyush Goyal who is increasingly emerging as a powerful Minister holds several portfolios like Food, Consumer Affairs and Public Distribution, Civil Aviation, and New and Non-Renewable Energy, the Power Minister is Raj Kumar Singh, R.K.Singh, Former Minister of State for Agriculture Sanjeev Kumar Balyan is now the Minister of State for Fisheries, Dairying and Animal Husbandry while Secunderabad MP former Minister of State for Home G.Kishen Reddy got a promotion and is now Union Minister for Tourism, Sports, Youth and Culture. And Anurag Thakur, former Minister of State for Finance is now Minister of State for Urban Development and Sports. So is former Minister of State for Home Affairs Kiren Rijiju, a native of Arunachal Pradesh, who is now Minister of State for Sports. While Ajit Dave is the Minister of State for Defense and prominent businessman and BPL Chairman Rajeev Chandrashekhar is the IT, Telecommunications and Skill Development(an interesting combination of portfolios in itself) Minister(whose inclusion is an attempt by the Prime Minister to draw on business acumen) in the new look Cabinet, many old faces have been retained like Sadhvi Rithambara Jyoti who continues to hold the Minister of State for Food Processing Industries portfolio. Gen. V.K.Singh is the Minister for Road Transport, Highways and Shipping while Ashwini Kumar Choubey, Buxar M.P. is the Union Minister for Health and Family Welfare. Former Minister of State for Shipping Mansukh. L Mandaviya is now the Minister of State for Health and Family Welfare while former Permanent Representative to the UN Hardeep Singh Puri and Alphons.J.Kannanthoman continue to be the Ministers of State for Urban Development, Housing, Civil Aviation and Energy and Petroleum and Minister of State for Tourism, Electronics and IT. Shripad Yesso Naik is the AYUSH(Ayurveda, Yoga, Unani, Siddha and Homeopathy) Minister. This is but a sprinkling of the Ministers of what is a bloated and elephantine Cabinet. A powerful Minister, Patna Sahib M.P. and former Union Minister for Law and Justice, Telecommunications, Electronics and IT Ravi Shankar Prasad has been retired.

Lok Sabha Speakers

The incumbent Lok Sabha Speaker is Om Birla two time M.P. and three time M.L.A. from Kota Bandi, Rajasthan who started off hs career as a youth leader of the BJP. The first Lok Sabha Speaker was M.A.Ayyangar who was followed by a long retinue of distinguished Speakers like Ganesh Vasudev Mavalankar, K.S.Hegde who was M.P. of the iconic South Bangalore Constituency, Somnath Chatterjee who never lost an election except one to Mamta Banerjee, the longest serving Speaker, former Agriculture Minister Balram Jakhar, Chattisgarh Administrator Shivraj Patil, Purushottam. A. Sangma who is a former Chief Minister of Meghalaya whose eldest son, Conrad Kongkal Sangma is the present Chief Minister of Meghalaya, Indore M.P. Sumitra Mahajan who in 1987 in a giant felling act defeated then Madhya Pradesh Chief Minister Prakash Chandra Sethi and got elected to the Lok Sabha and of course the present Speaker Om Birla and others.

Lok Sabha Deputy Speakers

The first Deputy Speaker of the Lok Sabha was M.A.Ayyangar who went on to become the first Speaker of the Lok Sabha, other Deputy Speakers include Raghnath Keshav Khadilkar, Shillong M.P. George Gilbert Swell, G.G.Swell, G.M.C.Balayogi of Andhra Pradesh who died in a helicopter crash, Shivraj Patil, Balram Jakhar, Chandigarh M.P. Charanjit Singh Atwal, Khunti M.P. Karia Munda, Tirupati M.P. R.Thambidurai and the post is currently TBD, vacant and others.

Pakistan

With regard to Pakistan, in view of Pakistan's importance to India, this writer will examine Pakistan's political structure in some depth. At the de facto apex(although the de jure head is the President of Pakistan), sits the Pak PM of which so far there have been 18, six of whom were assassinated(including the first Liaquat Ali Khan who staffed his cabinet with distinguished and senior civil servants and others), seven were sacked and 3 were deposed in coups. Pak PMs include the mild mannered, pliable and docile Mohammed Khan Junejo under hatchet man Zia ul-Haq whom Indians love to hate, the Oxford educated Farooq Leghari, Shah Mehmood Quereshi, not to mention the world famous examples of Zulfiqar Ali Bhutto who was hanged by General Zia ul Haq, Bhutto's daughter Benazir Bhutto who was assassinated and whose son Bilawal Bhutto now heads her party, the Pakistan Peoples Party(PPP), the now in the slammer Nawaz Sharif, Mr.Sharif's successor, former Railway and Petroleum Minister,the engineer politician, Dr.Shahid Khaqan Abbasi, the caretaker PM the jurist Nasir ul-Mulk who oversaw suspect elections in which Imran Khan polevaulted himself into the PMs seat in what was a neat judicial coup.

Pak Presidents include the first Gen.Iskander Mirza, Ghulam Ishaq Khan, the more famous examples of Asif Ali Zardari, Nawaz Sharif's bete noire, Gen. Pervez Musharraf, the bland Mamnoon Hussein and the incumbent Arif Alvi whose father Habib Alvi, in a quirk of fate, was Nehru's dentist. Then, of course, there is the Qaid-e-Azam, Mohammed Ali Jinnah, a man whose achievements have always been overshadowed by the world famous Nehru-Gandhi.

The current(the second one) Imran Khan Ministry[the Pak cabinet[Kabina e-Pakistan in Urdu] derives its power from Article 81(D) of the Pakistani Constitution] consists of 25 Federal Ministers, 5 Ministers of State and 6 Advisors most of whom took office on 20th August 2019. The Ministers are as follows: Shah Mehmood Quershi,

Foreign Minister, Asad Umar, Finance Minister, former Khyber Pakhtunwa Chief Minister Pervez Khattak, Defense Minister, former Railway Minister Sheikh Rasheed, Interior Minister, Minister of State for Interior Sheryar Khan Afridi, Farogh Naseem, Law and Justice Minister, Tariq Basheer Cheema, Housing and Works Minister, Shafqat Mehmood, Minister for Education and Professional Training, Literary Heritage, and National History, former Ambassador to the United States, Shireen Mazari, Human Rights Minister, Minister of Defense Production, the long standing Zubeida Jalal Khan who survived 4 cabinet reshuffles, and is now thriving in the 2nd Imran Khan Ministry[a former leading woman member of the Prime Minister Shaukat Aziz(a former Citibank Vice President, Mr.Aziz was PM for a brief while in 2002) Cabinet, Ms Khan belongs to the Balochistan Awami Party(BAP)], Minister of Health Aamir Mehmood Kaini(as part of the first Imran Khan Ministry), Minister for Inter-Provincial Coordination Fahmida Mirza, Minister of Information Fawad Chaudary, Minister of Information Technology and Telecommunications Khalid Maqbool Siddiqui, Minister of Petroleum Ghulam Sarwar Khan, Sheikh Rasheed Ahmed(as part of the 1st Imran Khan Ministry), Minister of Railways, Ali Haider Zaidi, Minister for Maritime Affairs, former Khyber Pakhtunwa CM Sardar Inayatullah Khan Gandapur, Minister for Kashmir Affairs and Gilgit-Baltistan, Khusro Bakhtiar, Minister for Science and Technology, Izaj Ahmed Shah, Minister for Railways, Omar Ayub Khan, Minister for Petroleum and so on. While former Pak High Commissioner to India Sohail Mehmood is the Foreign Secretary, Mian Asad Hayaud Din is the Secretary, Petroleum Ministry.

Going back to the Prime Minister Dr.Shahid Khaqan Abbasi, who did his Doctorate in Electrical Engineering from George Washington University, United States and is a former Railway and Petroleum Minister, government some of the Ministers include Defense Minister Khurram Dastgir Khan, Finance Minister Ishaq Dar and Minister of State for Finance Miftah Ismail, Khwaja Mohammed Asif who held the Foreign and Defense portfolios respectively and who threatened to nuclear way lay India, Minister of Interior Affairs, Capital Administration and Narcotics Control Ahsan Iqbal, Minister for Education, Professional Training, National History and Literary Heritage, Baligh-ur Rehman, Ali Haider Zaidi, Minister for Maritime Affairs, Minister for Inter-Provincial Coordination Riaz Hussein Pirzada, Minister for Industries and Production Ghulam Murtaza Jatoi, Minister of Parliamentary Affairs Sheikh Aftab Ahmed, Minister for Housing and Works Akram Khan Durrani, Minister for States and Frontier Regions(SAFFRON) Abdul Qadir Baloch, Minister for Water Resources Syed Javed Ali Shah, Minister of Religious Affairs and Inter-Faith Harmony Sardar Mohammed Youssef, Minister of Communications Hafiz Abdul Kareem, Minister of Power Awais Leghari, Minister of Statistics Kamran Michael, Minister of Climate Change Mushahid Ullah Khan, Minister of Railways Khwaja Saad Rafique, Minister of Maritime Affairs Hasil Bijenzo, Minister of Health, Health Services and Regulation Saira Afzal Tarar, Federal Minister of Commerce and Textiles Mohammed Pervez Malik, Federal Minister of Human Rights Mumtaz Ahmed Tarar, Federal Minister of Postal Services Maulana Ameer Zaman, Federal Minister of HRD and Overseas Pakistanis Pir Sadruddin Shah, Federal Minister of Privatisation Daniyal Aziz, Federal Minister of Food Security and Research Sikandar Hayat Khan Bosan, Federal Minister of Narcotics Control Salahuddin Tirmizi, Federal Minister of Defense Production Rana Tanveer Hussein, Federal Ministers of Justice Zahid Hamid and Mohammed Zakaullah. Then, there are the Ministers of State like Minister of State for Information and Broadcasting, National History and Literary Heritage Murriyum Aurangazeb, Minister of State for Petroleum Jam Kamal Khan(later Balochistan CM), Minister of Overseas Pakistanis and Human Resource Development(HRD) Abdul Rehman Khan Kanju, Minister of State for Power Abid Sher Ali, Minister of State for Maritime Affairs Chaudary Jaffar Iqbal, Minister of State of IT and Telecommunications Anusha Rehman, Ministers of State for Climate Change and Food Security and Research Ghalib Khan and

Syed Ayaz Ali Shah Sheerazi respectively, Minister of State of Science and Technology Mir Dostain Khan Domki, Minister of State for Finance Rana Afzal Tarar, Minister of State of Religious Affairs and Inter-Faith Harmony Mohammed Amin Ul-Hasnat Shah, Minister of State of Communications Muhammed Junaid Anwar Chaudary, Minister of State of Inter-Provincial Coordination Darshan Punshi, Minister of State for Interior Affairs and Capital Administration Mohammed Tallal Chaudary, Minister of State of Industries Arshad Leghari, Minister of State for Commerce and Textiles Akram Ansari, Minister of State of Human Rights Usman Ibrahim and others.

After Mr. Abbasi came Interim Prime Minister Nasir-ul- Mulk, a former Chief Justice of the Pakistan Supreme Court under whom Foreign and Defense Minister was former Pak Ambassador to UN Abdullah Hussein Haroon, Shamshad Akhtar was Finance Minister, Interior Minister was Azam Khan and among other key portfolios, the Law and Justice portfolio was held by Syed Zafar Ali Shah apart from other Ministers. Then came Mr. Nawaz Sharif who in a judicial coup under Article 61(f) of the Pakistani Constitution[under which an MP is declared unfit to hold public office if he is of dubious moral character(a reference to the Panama papers scandal that shook Pakistan)] was evicted from office and Mr. Imran Khan foisted himself onto the nation. In his power hunt as he powered his way through, Mr. Khan tried it all, anti-establishment, pro-establishment, left, right and center. Indeed, Mr. Khan pulled many rabbits from his hat. Interestingly, and in what ur a matter of huge satisfaction for India, dreaded terrorist Hafiz ur-Rehman's(who is wanted by India) party drew a blank in the elections which saw Mr.Imran Khan become Pak PM. While 172 is the magic figure in the Pak Parliament, 60 seats are reserved for women and 10 seats are reserved for religious and other minorities. The second Imran Khan Ministry is more or less the same as the first except for a minor reshuffle in which Faisal Vawda, Water Resources Minister, Water Resources Secretary was sacked and a few other minor adjustments were effected as seen earlier.

Interior Ministers of Pakistan, a key portfolio in any country, include the first Fazl-ur-Rehman, the second Khwaja Shahabuddin, Zakir Hussein, Abdus Sattar, President General Ayub Khan during whose time the Interior Ministry was known as the Home Ministry, PM Zulfikar Ali Bhutto, first President Gen.Iskander Mirza, Air Marshal Inam ul-Haq, Mohammed Khan Junejo, General Naseerullah Babar, General Mohinuddin Haider, General Mohammed Khan Khattak, Mahmood Haroon, Rehman Malik, Habib Khan(caretaker), Chaudary Nisar Ali Khan, Faisal Fayez, Omar Khan Afridi(caretaker) and others.

Past Pak Foreign Ministers include the consumately sophisticated Shahebzada Yakub Khan with who then Foreign Minister Narasimha Rao took calibrated steps towards that elusive Indo-Pak peace and amity, Hina Rabbani Khar, Khurshid Mohammed Kasuri, Sartaj Aziz(also Finance Minister), Mushahid Hussein who rather grandoisely and gratuously proclaimed "had India solved the Kashmir problem, Shashi Tharoor would be Secretary General today", the incumbent Shah Mehmood Quereshi and a galaxy of glitterati.

Coming to the Chief Ministers of Pakistan, Pakistan has six provinces: Punjab, Balochistan, Khyber Pakhtoonwa[formerly North West Frontier Province(NWFP)], Sind, what Pakistan calls Azad Kashmir and what India calls Pak. Occupied Kashmir(POK) and Gilgit-Baltistan. Penning a new note, Pakistan's lawmakers a few years back carried out some constitutional rearrangements with regard to Gilgit-Baltistan controversially integrating the disputed areas into the Pak Union. Pakistan also has nine Federally Administered Tribal Areas(FATAs) like the Orakzai Tribal Area, Bijnaur Federally Administered Tribal Area, North Wazirstan, South Wazirstan and so on. These areas are considered volatile and dangerous even by the Pakistan government and the Pak. government in its own travel advisories advises foreign visitors to avoid travelling to these areas.

In so far as the Chief Ministers of Pakistan are considered, the incumbent CMs are as follows: Pakistan Punjab-Sardar Usman

Buzdar(predecessor Nawaz Sharif's son Shabaz Sharif. In fact, consequent upon Shabaz Sharif coming into his own in national mainstream politics as a wild card entry for the Wazir-e-Azam's post, Mr.Shabaz Sharif's son Hamza Sharif who came within a whisker of the Punjab CMs mantle but not quite was to have taken over as Punjab CM, but, both were vain bids and were like clutching at straws in the wind, groping in the dark with no light at the end of the tunnel and the bids fell flat on their face as a judicial coup shook and overtook Pakistan as the honourable judges went berserk) Balochistan-Mir Abdul Quddus Bizenjo(predecessors Pervez Khattak and Jam Kamal Khan respectively) who is a member of the Provincial Assembly of Balochistan and the Cabinet of Balochistan, Khyber Pakhtoonwa- Mahmood Khan, POK-Raja Farook Haider Khan, Sind-Murad Ali Shah, the disputed areas of Gilgit-Baltistan-Hafiz Hafeez ur-Rehman. The CM is the political agent of the President of Pakistan in the province or State. Some of the other former CMs that come to mind are: Khyber Pakhtoonwa-Sardar Inayatullah Khan Gandar, Justice Tariq Aziz, Fazal Ali, current Defense Minister Pervez Khattak, the first CM Abdul Qayyum Khan, Aftab Ahmed Sherpao, the incumbent's predecessor Masood Khan and a long list of other distinguished CMs some of whom were civil servants like the present CM Mahmood Khan who had a long distinguished career in the Pak. foreign services and served in a raft of diplomatic assignments including as Pak. Ambassador to Russia and many, many others to name only a few. And holding 0.0% of the world's oil reserves most of which are found in the Potohar Plateau in Punjab, Pakistan ranks 52nd in world Petroleum production.

Sri Lanka

The Rajapaksa family led by its brothers duo, elder brother Gotabaya Rajapaksa, currently President and a former Defense Secretary and younger brother Mahinda Rajapaksa, currently Prime Minister(and a former President) wields enormous influence in Sri Lanka. Former Presidents and PMs include President Maithripala Sirisena[Sri Lanka Freedom Party(SLFP)], PM Ranil Wickramasinghe[United National Party(UNP)] during whose tenure Sri Lanka was wracked by spiraling unemployment, severe drought and was beset with a host of other problems, first woman Prime Minister of the world Sirimavo Badaranaike whose husband was also a former Prime Minister of Sri Lanka and incidentally when Ms. Bandaranaike took charge in 1965, there was a debate across the world as to how to address a female PM, Madam PM or ? etc as till then no woman had become PM. Ms Bandaranaike(whose daughter Chandrika Kumaratunge is a former President) held the PM's post from 1965-69 and then again from 1971-77 and 1994-99 Other Sri Lankan Prime Ministers include the person who along with Rajiv Gandhi signed in the Indo-Sri Lankan Peace Accord and signed out and snuffed out Rajiv Gandhi's life, J.H.Jayawardene. The tumoultous events that led to the entry of the IPKF into Sri Lanka and the subsequent civil war that wracked Sri Lanka from 1972 to 2002 and that turned Sri Lanka's insides inside out are too well known to need enumeration here. Suffice it to say, as anyone seeing T.V. will understand, why LTTE leader Balasingham became billi singham when faced with the T.V. cameras! Actually, the political trajectory of the Sri Lankan Tamils is different from the Indian Tamils although it is understable that Indian Tamils sympathize with their cousins in Sri Lanka who are stuck in the killing fields of Sri Lanka and a closer look at Sri Lanka's demographic composition shows up the cracks and fissures running down the faultlines of Sri Lanka. And the LTTE in its time was designated the most dangerous terrorist organisation in the world with recourse to a surprising array of resources.And lest the world forget that Sri Lanka is not just about Tamils, a Telugu candidate was thrown in a previous election mix queering the pitch for Tamil candidates but also at the same time adding color to the campaign.

In 1987, Sri Lanka's Tamil majority Northern Province was hived off into Northern and North Eastern Provinces and again remerged and reintegrated in 2007, now under the able guidance of CM

Canagasabhapathy Visuvalingam Wigneswaran and Governor Reginald Cooray. Cabinet Ministers of the Northern Province include Education, Social and Cultural Affairs Minister Kandiah Sarveswaran and others. Apart from the Northern Province, other Provinces of Sri Lanka include Eastern Province, Western Province, Southern Province, South Central Province, South Eastern Province, South Western Province etc. And Mr.Mathripala Sirisena during a visit to New Delhi cited the economy, drought, the bond crisis and Mr.Wickremasinghe attack on Mr.Sirisena for going slow on Indian projects in Sri Lanka as the reasons for falling out with Mr.Wickramasinghe as an increasing number of Sri Lankans rue New Delhi's "Viceroy approach" to Sri Lanka.

The Sri Lankan Parliament Speaker is Yapa Maha Abeywardena who is preceded in the post by Karu Jayasurya who in his letter to then Sri Lankan President Maithripala Sirisena noted pro-rogation and suspension of Parliament had to be in consultation with the Speaker and or even in case of dismissal of the PM and the appointment of the a powerful national figure as PM as happened in the case of PM Ranil Wickramasinghe and former President Mahinda Rajapaksa who backs the Sri Lanka Podujana Peramuna or Sri Lanka Peoples Party which did rather well in the Municipal elections and Urban local bodies(ULBs) elections held in Sri Lanka, the Speaker had to be taken into confidence.

As far back as 2016, Mr.Rajapaksa had predicted he would topple the government of the Mathripala Sirisena-Ranil Wickramasinghe combine, something which he did in 2018, elder brother Gotabatya Rajapaksa foisting himself into the President's chair as Mr.Rajapaksa Jr eased himself into the PM's saddle striking a back room deal with Mr.Sirisena which prompted the latter to pull the plug on the Rajapaksa duo, stunning the country(and the world). But, paper tiger Sirisena is a spent force and he poses no threat to the powerful Rajapaksa duo who seem to be masters of all they survey in Sri Lanka. Finance and Media Minister Mangala Samaraweera called the deft move by the wily Rajapaksa brothers as nothing short of a coup in a tweet.

Among Foreign Ministers, the incumbent is Dinesh Gunawardena who was preceded by Tilak Marapana, Mangala Samaraweera also a one time Finance Minister(SLFP), Rohita Bogologamma(UNP), G.L.Pieris(SLFP), J.Jayawardena, Sirimavo Bandaranayake, Anura Bandaranayake, S.W.R.D.Bandaranayake, the inaugural holder, Sir Dudley.H. Senanayake and others.

Water, Drainage and Sewarage Ministers include Vimala Jayawardena and others. Oil Ministers include the incumbent Udaya Prabath Gammanpila and his predecessor Arjuna Ranatunga. While Duminda Dissanayake is the Deputy Minister for Petroleum, Gammina Lokuge is the Minister for Power, New and Non-Renewable Energy.

Going back to the previous Maithripala Sirisena-Ranil Wickramasinghe combo Ministry, Urban Development, Town Planning, Electricity, Science and Technology, Atomic Energy and Environment and Climate Change Minister is Champika Ranawaka of the Paatige Hettaiah Rachi or Sri Lanka National Heritage Party, a right wing leader who was arrested and released, Law and Order Minister Ranjit Madduma Bandara(former Law and Justice Ministers include Mr.Ranil Wickramasinghe himself and Sagala Ratnayake), and Talatha Atukorale is the Justice Minister. Sajitha Premadasa is Hambantota MP. Mr.Premadasa spent much of his early career esp. in the early 70s and late 80s in armed left wing extremist movements. So as can be seen from the fine print, the Maithripala Sirisena-Ranil Wickramasinghe government was a curious, most inorganic, unnatural, unscientific and illogical alliance of left wing and right wing elements, a group of rhinos and tigers who were bound to fall out and what with the wily Rajapaksa brothers driving between a wedge between them and playing spoilsport, it soon collapsed and fell like a pack of cards, a row of dominoes.

And as regards Humbantota port, while India viewed it as a white elephant, China saw its geo-strategic merit and heft, invested in it, cultivated it and acquired it as a base, in the process acquiring a base right at India's doorstep much to India's dismay. China also constructed Sri Lanka's tallest tower, the Lotus Tower in Colombo. Why, China has many ongoing projects in India itself even as the country sources some 64% of its imports from China. India needs to look into this. The move to ban some 115 Chinese apps, apps like CamScanner, Beidou Map, ClubFactory etc. which gives positions on China's BRI initiative in response to the India-China armed skirmishes was a step in the right direction. But, it was a knee jerk reaction and India needs to take proactive, sustained and continued action in this direction if it is to contain the dragon's threat as the countries of the world go about shunning China, a country whose government suppresses its own people.

Nepal

From 1758 all Nepali Prime Ministers were Chetris except Raganath Poduyal who was a Brahmin. The nobility of the Gurkhas was descended from the aristocracy. These Bharadars or high officials comprised the elite ruling class. There were castes such as Pandes, Chetris, Gurkhas, Ranas and others. The different Prime Ministers of Nepal include Damodar Pande, Maitrika Prasad Koirala. Tanka Prasad Acharya, Surya Bahadur Thapa, Baburam Bhattarai, Girija Prasad Koirala, Sushil Kumar Koirala, King Gyanendra, Sher Bahadur Deuba, Pushpa Kumar Dahal alias Prachanda, a centrist who backed a Marxist-Leninist coalition led by former Prime Minister Khadga Prasad Sharma Oli, K.P.Sharma Oli, incumbent Prime Minister Sher Bahadur Deuba II and others. Speakers include the powerful Krishna Bahadur Mahara(a one time Home and Communications Minister and Rolpa MP who cut his teeth in the Marxist movemement) who however had to put in his papers in a unseemly sex scandal involving one of his female staffers, Agni Prasad Sapkota, the first female Speaker Onsari Gharti Magar who took charge in 2013, Deputy Speaker Shivmaya Thumbahampe, Finance Ministers include Yuba Raj Khetiwada, Foreign Ministers include Pradeep Kumar Gyawali who once along with Chinese Foreign Minister Wang Yi talked of India, China and Nepal playing tango and ping pong diplomacy and profiting from China's BRI Initiative even as Mr.Yi referrering to India and China spoke of 1+1 being equal to 11. But, these are mere words and there is a fundamental conflict of interest between India and China. China views India as its competitor and rival. Things will not improve unless China stops viewing India through the border dispute prism.Foreign Secretaries include Shankar Das Bairagi, his predecessor Dilip Bhattarai and others. The traditionally India-friendly Nepalese who were seen as a buffer between India and China are now practicing a fine balancing act between India and China and walking a tightrope to India's dismay. In this, the Chinese Ambassador in Khatmandu, Ms.Hou Yanqi who has a rather sleazy ugly underbelly is playing a proactive role and the United States Ambassador to Nepal, Roger Berry recently revealed that the Dalai Lama's birthday celebrations were cancelled in Nepal allegedly at Chinese insistence. But, even today Nepal(esp. the Terrai regions of Uttar Pradesh and Bihar), to a great measure serves as a buffer between India and China though Nepal through its Ambassador in Delhi, Neel Kanth Uprety, a former Chief Election Commissioner let it be known to New Delhi it would not brooke Indian interference in Nepalese affairs. The President is Bidya Devi Bhandari and she was preceded by Ram Baran Yadav and the Pratinidhi Sabha is the Parliament.

Bangladesh

Foreign Ministers include the incumbent, Abul Kalam Abdul Momin, Abul Hassan Mahmud Ali, Sheikh Hasina, Dipu Moni, Iftekhar Ahmed Chaudary, Ijaduddin Ahmed, Morshed Khan, Minister of State for Foreign Affairs, Shahryar Khan, Humayun Akhtar Chaudary, Prof.Mohammed Shamsul Haq, Abu Sayeed Chaudary, Kamal Hossein, Abdus Samad Azad, the first Foreign Minister Khondakar Mushtaq Ahmed who was in office from April 1971 to December 1971 during a nascent stage in Bangladesh's history and many other disinguished glitterarti.

The Bangladeshi Home Minister is Asadussaman Khan Kamal. The Roads, Highways and Bridges Minister is Obaidul Qadeer while Engineer Musharraf Hussein is the PWD Minister in the Cabinet headed by Prime Minister Sheikh Hasina, the Agriculture Minister is Abdul Razak, a former Education Minister is Dipu Moni, Information Minister is Hasanul Haq Inu among other Ministers. Incidentally, the incumbent Foreign Minister's predecessor Mr. Abul Hassan Mahmud Ali is a former Disaster Management and Relief Minister. Bangladesh's founder first President, the legendary Sheikh Mujibur Rehman whose daughter is the incumbent Prime Minister was conferred Asia's version of the Peace Nobel, the prestigious Gandhi Peace Prize for the year 2020 for his monumental contributions to Bangladesh and World Peace shortly ahead of Bangladesh Golden Jubilee year and 50th Indepenence Anniversary. In recent times, Bangladesh has been headed by the duo of current Prime Minister Sheikh Hasina of the Awami League and the Bangladesh National Party(BNP)'s jailed leader(jailed for graft, but the move could be a ploy to keep her out of power, whatever, the two Begums are proving to the bane of Bangladesh) Begum Khaleda Zia whose London based son Tarique Rehman is leading the BNP in Ms Zia's absence and Ms Zia may even be grooming her son to be her successor in yet another South Asian example of dynastic rule, Bangladesh being the only country in the world where there is a woman PM and woman principal Opposition Leader, the principal contenders for the top job being women and a woman Chairperson of Parliament. Mirza Fazlur Rehman is Mr.Rehman's predecessor BNP President while Shamsusaman Khan Kamal is the Secretary General of the BNP. Foreign secretaries include the inaugural holder, Abul Fateh, Shahidul Haq, Shafikur Rehman the current officeholder, Masud Bin Momin and others. Bangladeshi Ambassador to Myanmar is Mohammed Safihuir Rehman. Bangladesh's Parliament is the Jatiya Sansad.

Maldives

With an area of 298 sq km and population of 3.4 million, Maldives is one of the smallest countries in the world, both area wise and population wise. It is so small an island cluster that during the 2002 tsunami for one terrifying moment it seemed the entire of Maldives would go down under. Which is why Maldives is one of the few countries in the world which has bought land abroad as a possible future destination for its population to emigrate in case of a similar emergency occurring.

Presidents of Maldives include the incumbent, Ibrahim Mohammed Solih, popularly known as 'Ibu' who was born in Hinnavaru, Maldives, his predecessor, Abdullah Yameen Abdul Gayoom who surprisingly conceded defeat in elections paving the way for Mr.Solih, a joint opposition candidate(backed by the Jumhoorie Party, the Maldivian Democratic Party of former India leaning President Mohammed Nasheed who said the new dispensation would continue the Maldivian government's traditional "India first" policy, and a rival faction of President Abdullah Yameen's Progressive Party of Maldives) to take over, other officeholders include Mohammed Waheed Hassan(in whose cabinet present Maldivian Ambassador to Sri Lanka Mohammed Hussein Shareef was HRD, Cultural and Social Affairs Minister, Ambassador to Japan and government spokesperson),Mohammed Nasheed, now Speaker of Maldives Parliament, Maumoon Abdul Gayoom(whose son Farid Gayoom is an M.P.) and others. Maldives's national script is the Dhihevi Script.

Foreign Ministers

Foreign Ministers of Maldives include Hasan Farid Didi, Mohammed Amin Didi, Ibrahim Famyudheri Kilegefanu, Ibrahim Nasir, Ahmed Zaki, Fatullah Jameel, Ahmed Shaheed Abdullah Shahid, Ahmed Shaheed, Abdullah Shaheed, Abdul Samad Abdullah, Acting Foreign Minister Asim Ahmed, Ahmed Naseem,

Marriyum Shakeelah, Duniya Maumoon, Mohammed Asim, and the incumbent, Abdullah Shahid. Mohammed Shainee is a former Agriculture and Fisheries Minister.

Afghanistan

Afghanistan is presently in a state of flux and is stuck in a quagmire and stasis after the Taliban overran the country after the phased withdrawl of American, British and NATO troops from the landlocked country beginning 2014. There currently exists a power vaccum with no government in place, democratic or otherwise. Prior to that, under the deal that the Taliban struck with the West, the Taliban for its part, would have to abjure violence, respect the rights of Afghan men and women and fall within the ambit of the Afghan constitution with America, Britain, NATO, China, Russia and Pakistan(a country that is very active in Afghanistan) and, of course, the Taliban being parties to the deal in return for the full, phased withdrawl of Western troops. India, too, is contructively engaged in Afghanistan(a country with which its national interest coincides) like, for instance, in the construction of the Salma Dam which among other things provides electricity to Afghans and the Border Roads Organisation(BRO) is also very active in Afghanistan building roads, bridges and railways and according to unconfirmed reports, India is training Afghan pilots in the Beira Corridor. But as a senior American diplomat warned "the road ahead is full of thorns and the deal could come apart with Afghanistan falling into a endless vortex of violence". And that's exactly what happened. The government of President Mohammed Ashraf Ghani couldn't survive the crisis and fell the President fleeing the country with "hardly enough time to put my shoes on". Fundamentalism seems to be the opium of the Mullahs and Maulvis in Afghanistan and Afghanistan is stuck in a quagmire, a quicksand which is slowly sucking the country in.

In the government of President Ashraf Ghani(whom many Afghans wanted gone and this led to the popularity of mercenary executive Erik Prince of Blackwater security firm fame). The United States and NATO forces during their time were led by Generals such as General Scott Miller, General John Nicholson and the very first Commander Stanley Allen McChrystal, U.S. Army War College and U.S. Army Infantry School and decorated with the Bronze Star medal who assumed command on June 15, 2009(when the Americans overran Afghanistan. From the Americans to the Taliban which took over after the Americans threw in the towel. Whew! What a journey!) and since 2010, the Afghan Mission Network became a rallying point and the primary information sharing platform for U.S. and NATO troops in Afghanistan in support of Gen.McChrystal's game plan and counter-insurgency campaign. Also, the Generals in the Pentagon emerged from the woodwork convinced there was a goldmine beneath the landmines in Afghanistan. In the cabinet of President Ashraf Ghani, Salahuddin Rabbani was the Foreign Minister and Wais Barmak was the Interior Minister while another minister Waheed Majroh has since been sacked by the Taliban. He was the last minister of the erstwhile democratically elected government to have been sacked so.

In Mr.Ghani's Cabinet, Abdul Rashid Dostum was the First Vice President while former Foreign Minister Abdullah Abdullah was the Chief Executive. Mohammed Ahmed is the Governor of one of the Afghan provinces and the United States dropped "the mother of all bombs" the GUB118 and other similar such bunker buster bombs on Taliban strongholds, underground tunnels and terror dens in Nagarhar province in Afghanistan apart from resorting to other draconian measures in a bid to eliminate the Taliban. The Haqqani network apart from, of course, the Taliban and other similar splinter groups are the terrorist organisations currently active in Afghanistan. Any fragmentation of Afghanistan will have a centrifugal impact on the unity of Pakistan. Other Afghan Presidents include Mr. Ghani's predecessor, the Shimla educated Hamid Karzai, Dr. Sigbatullah Mojadidi, Soviet stooge Dr.Mohammed Zafarullah who died a gory death in the Afghan Embassy in Washington where he had taken refuge after fleeing from Afghanistan allegedly having been killed by the Taliban, Akram Kamal and others. On 1 December 1980, Soviet armored columns thundered into Afghanistan and the Russians installed their puppet, Mohammed Zafarullah in Kabul and Afghanistan broke up into a long period of civil war, strife and unrest where the American backed Mujahideen played a key role in opposing the Soviets through American and Mujahidden Army and Air Force bases such as the Bagram Air Base from where American fighter bombers took off to bomb Soviet targets in Afghanistan. Regional warlords like Gulbuddin Hekmatyar and Abdul Rashid Dostum threw a spanner into the troubled waters of Afghanistan. Afghanistan's troubles seem to be never ending with this time it being the turn of the dreaded Taliban to have its say in Kabul. The Afghan Interior Minister in the Hamid Karzai Cabinet was Hanif Atmar.

The Afghan Parliament is the Loyajirga in the elections to which at the time of Mohammed Ashraf Ghani, in an important development, Afghanistan's Ambassador to India, Shaida Mohammed Abdali submitted his resignation to Mr.Ghani during the latter's visit to India ostensibly to take part in the elections.

Bhutan

Bhutan's Prime Minister is Dr.Lotay Tshering while the King is Yigme Khesar Namgyel Wangchuk whose predecessor was his father, Yigme Singye Wangchuk while the present Queen is Jetsun Pema. The Indian Ambassador in Thimpu, Ms.Ruchira Kamboj, a former Ambassador to South Africa and UNESCO, is playing her due role in Bhutan so that Bhutan doesn't become another Nepal and continues to be a buffer between India and China. The Egyptian Ambassador to India and Bhutan, Dr.Heba Eldin Elmarassi is putting in efforts to keep her country's ties with India and Bhutan cordial and friendly. Nepal and Bhutan, notably Bhutan, act as a buffer between India and China and the Indo-Tibetan Border Police(ITBP) which was created in the aftermath of the 1962 Chinese aggression to guard the 4,448km border between India and China, the longest disputed border in the world, under the able guidance of its DG R.K.Pachnanda is keeping a silent vigil along the entire long border.

Tibet(China)

As is well known, Tibet is an autonomous region of China. But, a Tibetan government-in-exile, the second oldest in the world [after the Belarus Parliament-in-exile, the Rada(whose Speaker is Ivonka Survilla), which is exiled in Ottawa, Canada after the Red Army overran Belarus in 1920] exists in Dharmasala, Shimla, India where the Dalai Lama took refuge after India granted him political asylum in 1959 on condition that he would not indulge in political activities against China after he fled from China as a 15 year old boy fearing Chinese persecution and he has since stayed over in India. India will never admit it, but it will do nothing to disturb the Dalai Lama out of India. Now the hunt is on for a new Dalai Lama and Speaker of the US House of Representatives, Nancy Pelosi, has asked China to keep its butt out of this. Several names are doing the rounds with the frontrunner being the 17th Karmapa, Urgyen Trinley Dorjee or Ogyen Trinley Dorjee who follows the Dalai Lama and the 14th Karmapa apart from others. His brother is Jetsun Pelzom. But, a dark horse could very likely emerge. Quite probable.

The Speaker of the Tibetan government-in-exile(Parliament) is the newly elected Khenpo Sonam Tenphel who was elected 2021and Dolma Tsering is the Deputy Speaker while Dawa Tsering is the Interim Deputy Speaker before whom the Deputy Speaker was Acharya Yeshi Phuntsok. Recently, Jharkhand CM Hemant Soren had a tete a te with Mr.Phuntsok.

VII

West Asia(or Middle East as the British like to call it)

Saudi Arabia

Saudi ageing King, 83 year old(getting to be 84) King Salman is because of his advanced age, only a titular head. The real power center is his ambitious son, the powerful Prince Mohammed bin Salman bin Abdul Aziz Al Saud of the House of Saud who is so autocratic that he "arrested" the then Lebanese Prime Minister, Saad Hariri(who has since made way for Hassan Diab) and had him bought to Riyadh but soon Mr.Hariri was back in Beirut and Iran backed Houthi rebels who played a key role in the entire murky affair claimed victory and the ambitious Prince had egg on his face. Not just that, in a royal purge in 2017-18, Prince Salman arrested several ministers, high officials and one prominent businessman, Al Waleed bin Talal who has interests in Citicorp., Twitter and owns 95% of the shares on the Saudi bourses. He did not spare even his mother whom he put under house arrest. The different Saudi

Foreign Ministers are as follows: incumbent Foreign Minister and former Ambassador to United States and Germany, Prince Faisal bin Farhan Al Saud, the world's second longest serving Foreign Minister[after former Austrian Foreign Minister Prince Klemens Wenzel Nepomuk Lothar von Matternich(who later became Chancellor in 1722) who served from 1709 to 1748 before the liberal revolutions of 1748 forced him out] Prince Salman bin Saud Al Mohammed bin Saud, Adel Ahmed Al Jubeir Adel Al Jubeir, Minister of State for Foreign Affairs Nizar bin Obaid Madani, Prince Faisal bin AbdulAziz Al Saud and others. And Khalid bin Ayyaf Al Muqrin who replaced Miteib bin Abdullah(who was arrested in the 2017-18 purge) is the Minister of the National Guard while Mohammed Al Tuwaijri is the Minister of Economy and Planning before whom the officeholder was Adel Fakeih(Adel Fakieh was one of the Ministers who was arrested by Prince Mohammed bin Salman alongwith Ministers like Mansour bin Muqrin who was earlier a Governor of Saudi Arabia's southern Asir Province. Mansour bin Muqrin has since been killed when the chopper he was fleeing the country in was bought down allegedly on orders of the Saudi Government). And Tamadar bin Youssef al Ramah, Deputy Minister for Social Development and Labor, is only the second woman Minister in the Cabinet of King Salman(read Prince Salman) in what is a highly conservative Kingdom. Another prominent woman face is in the diplomatic corps., Her Royal Highness Princess Reema Bint Bandar bin Sultan Al Saud, Saudi Ambassador to United States who is Saudi Arabia's only woman Ambassador. Otherwise, there are almost no woman faces in the conservative country's Cabinet. Saudi Kings who are the Custodians of the two Mosques include apart from King Salman, King Fahd, King Khalid, King Faisal bin Abdul Aziz Al Saud who took charge in 1913 and others. Saudi Oil Ministers include the incumbent Khalifa bin Salman Al Saud whose predecessor was Adel Zakeih, the respected Oil Minister Faisal Al Farhan, Khalifa bin Salman bin Saud and others. The Deputy Minister of Defense is Mohammed bin Abdullah Al Assay. Other Governors of Saudi Provinces include Nayef bin Mohammed, Salman bin Muhammed and others. Other former Ministers include Fahd bin Salman Al Saud and others. In fact, Prince Mohammed bin Salman's nephew, Mohammed bin Nayef bin Abdul Aziz Al Saud was the heir apparent, but in a royal coup, the ambitious Prince usurped power.

United Arab Emirates(UAE)

The UAE gained independence in 1970 and became a Federation of six Emirates, Abu Dhabi, the political capital, Dubai, the financial capital and richest Emirate, Ras Al Khaimah, Um Al Qaiwain, Ajman, Sharjah and the seventh Emirate, Fujairah joined the Federation in 1971. The President of UAE is Khalifa bin Zayed Al Nahyan of the Al Nahyan royal House and he is the also the ruler of Abu Dhabi. The Vice President is Khalifa bin Mohammed Al Saud. The Prime Minister is Mohammed bin Rashid Al Maktoum. The ruling royal Houses of the UAE include besides the Al Nahyan House, the Al Qassimi House, Al Maktoum House etc. The Foreign Minister is Khalifa bin Abdullah bin Zayed Al Nahyan and he is preceded in the position by former Ambassador to the United States, and Minister of State for Foreign Affairs and Minister for Federal National Council Affairs Anwar Mohammed Gargash, a Havard and Cairo University alumni. And Emirati Oil Minister in energy rich UAE is Suhail Muhammed Firaj Al Mazrouei. And former Nigerian Petroleum Minister Mohammed Sanusi Barkindo is OPEC(Organisation of Petroleum Exporting Countries) Secretary General. In recent years, the UAE has emerged as a significant space power launching the Al Aqsa(Hope Peace) Martian probe which among other things will probe Martian craters. And Hazza Al Mansouri became the first Emirati to go to space going to the ISS alongwith American astronaut, Jessica Meir piggyback on a Russian Soyuz rocket. The two developments took place in 2020 post-Mangalyaan. So, in a way, even minor powers like the UAE are stealing a march over India not to speak of major space powers like China which sent the Tiangyong 1 Mars probe post-Mangalyaan.

Bahrain

Bahrain's King is Hamad bin Isa bin Salman Al Khalifa while the Prime Minister is Salman bin Hamad bin Isa Al Khalifa and the Foreign Minister is Dr.Abdullahtif bin Rashid Al Zayani before whom the Foreign Minister was Khalifa bin Salman Al Khalifa who traces his origins to India and who, in fact, paid a visit to India a few years back. Before the incumbent PM, the Prime Minister was Hamad bin Isa bin Salman Al Khalifa who took charge in 1970 and who at the time was the longest serving PM in the world before he relinquished office in favor of his successor, the incumbent. Other Kings of Bahrain called by various titles like Kings, Hakims and Vaziers include Salman bin Isa Al Khalifa, Hamad bin Isa bin Salman Al Khalifa, Isa bin Salman Al Khalifa, Mohammed bin Salman Al Khalifa, Khalifa bin Mohammed Al Khalifa, Mohammed bin Khalifa Al Khalifa and others.

Kuwait

The King of Kuwait is Jaber Al Mubarak Al Sabah whose predecessor was Jaber Al Sabah Al Sabah. Other officeholders include Jaber Al Hamad Al Mubarak Al Sabah who also served as Minister of Defense before a court ordered his detention on corruption charges.

Oman

The Sutan of Oman is Haitham bin Tariq. A former Culture and Heritage Minister, his predecessor was his cousin Qaboos bin Said Al Said who was a bachelor and left no heir paving the way for his cousin and successor, the present Sultan. Another former Sultan of Oman is Tariq Al Aziz.

Qatar

The Emir of Qatar is Thamam bin Hamad Al Thani whose predecessor was Khalifa bin Thamam bin Hamad Al Thani who in turn was preceded by Mustafa bin Thamam bin Hamad Al Thani. Qatar is rich, Qatar has the world's best airline, Qatar has skyscrapers but sadly, Qatar has no trees. It is a total desert.

Israel

Israel was carved out of Palestine, an event which had international ramifications and the Arabs giving a shrill response talked of "driving the Jews into the sea", a vain boast, given the fact that the dispersed Arabs lack the concomitant military strength to carry out their threat. And, Israel today is a reality the Arabs will have to live with.

Israeli Prime Ministers include the first David Ben Gurion in whose honor Tel Aviv Airport is named, Golda Meir, an Ambassador to first the United Nations and later to the United States, Menachem Begin, Moshe Dayan, the socialist and moderate Shimon Peres whose entry was met with relief in Arab Capitals, Ehud Barak, the wily Benjamin Netanyahu whose successor is the incumbent Naftali Bennet and others. Presidents include the first Chaim Weizmann before whom David Ben Gurion was Chairman of the Provisional State Council, the second Yitzak Ben Zvi, Kadish Luz, Zalman Shazar, Yitzak Navon, Avraham Burg, Ezer Weizmann, General Chaim Herzog who was President of the UN General Assembly for the period ended 1975 and Israeli Ambassador to the United Nations from 1975 to 1977, Moshe Katsav, Shimon Peres, Reuven Revalin and the present President Issac Herzog who took charge in 2021. The former President Reuven Revalin who recently on his visit to India(as the first Israeli President to visit India) said "Israel had waited for 60 years for this move by India" a referral to the recognition of Israel by the right-wing BJP government in Delhi but not before the first deaths in India over India's foreign policy after an anti-Palestinian move by the prevailing dispensation in Delhi. The BJP answer to the Congress's traditional hostility towards

Israel is that like the United States, Israel and India are natural allies. As a reciprocal gesture to Mr.Revelin visit, Prime Minister Modi also paid a return visit to Israel. Mr. Netanyahu and Mr.Benny Ganzt, a politician belonging to the opposition Blue and White Party knocked out and cobbled together a power sharing agreement 2020 under which they would share the spoils of power with Mr.Ganzt taking charge as the country's Defense Minister and Mr.Netanyahu would continue as Prime Minister till Oct.2021 when Mr.Ganzt would become the Prime Minister(this Mr.Ganzt forced upon a reluctant Mr.Netanyahu by cornering him in the Knesset in terms of vote share). Mr.Ganzt did become Defense Minister but not Prime Minister. Instead, Mr.Naftali Bennet did. Under Mr.Netenyahu, Avigdor Lieberman, a hawk belonging to the Israel Beteanhu Party, served as Defense Minister in the first half of Mr.Netanyahu's Premiership(when he resigned in protest against Mr.Netanyahu's decision to enter into a ceasefire in the Gaza Strip) and Benny Ganzt served in the second half. Mr.Naftali Bennet himself a former Defense Minister, also served as Minister for Religious and Diaspora Affairs. He is now in the New Right and Moshe Kahlon was the Finance Minister in Mr.Netenyahu's Cabinet while Ms.Ayelet Shaked a Computer Engineer belonging to the New Right serving as Justice Minister. Other important Ministers include Minister for Intelligence, Strategic Affairs and Science and Technology Yisrael Katz, Minister for Public Security, Strategic Affairs and Information Gilad Menashe Erdan(Member of the Knesset for Likud) whom then British Secretary of International Development and Women and Equal Oppurtunities(and Northumberland MP) Penelope Mary 'Penny' Mordaunt met in a highly hush hush visit which costed her scalp and she had to put in her papers and others. Historically, Britain has been less tolerant of Israeli instrasigence than the latter's all weather and bell weather ally, America. Israel's relations with the United States have been like the tail wagging the dog, the tone and tenor for them set as they are by the powerful American Israeli Public Affairs Committee, a Jewish lobby in the United States, and backed by the large Jewish population in the United States.

America 2018 moved its Embassy in Israel from Tel Aviv to Jerusalem, the city being a bone of contention between Jews and Arabs as it is home to three religons-Islam, Judaism and Christianity and the American Ambassador to Israel, David Melech Friedman, a bankruptcy lawyer, is a known Palestinian baiter. The Islamic belief is that Prophet Mohammed ascended to heaven from the top of the Al-Aqsa Mosque in Jerusalem and as such the city and the shrine are the third holiest shrine to Muslims after Mecca and Medina.

The Scud that boomeranged-Iraq

Saddam Hussein-led Iraq scored a self goal when it fired Scuds[the Soviet launcher(in Western terminology Roland M III missile) that took the world by storm during the Gulf War of the early 90s] into Israel. America came to Israel's aid(with Bush Jr taking a personal interest in the war, in his words "the gall of that guy in Baghdad" "who tried to kill my father" an allegory to the assassination attempt on Bush Sr. by Saddam Hussein) and buried Saddam Hussein(with Bush Jr., that way a man known for his gaffes, even going graphic) with a side script that the entire war started with Baghdad invading Kuwait. The American Ambassador to Iraq at the start of the war was April Glaspie. How the American government deflected America's anger from Osama bin Laden to Saddam Hussein was the greatest PR conjuring trick in history. During the Gulf war a witch hunt was launched against liberal newspapers like the New York Times with one commentator saying "I can see Maureen Dowd waiting to use the word quagmire" and "liberals are like the Republican Guard, they never know when to quit". One cartoon summed it up "Gee, these people seem hostile to us and we haven't even got past New Jersey yet". Iraq which was for a long time in a stasis with de facto control being in American hands. Only now(2019) some semblance of normalcy is being restored. But, it all touch and go. In fact, before the discovery of oil in these areas way back in the 1920s, the countries of the Gulf were known only for their semantic value. And with the discovery of new oil fields in the

United States and Canada and the invention of new technologies like fracking and horizontal drilling the wheel may have turned full circle with the America-led West once again losing its interest in the countries of the Gulf with China filling the vaccum left by the West much to India's dismay. But, these are early days yet and the West's interest in the Gulf seems to be abiding, varied and continuing and this theory may prove to be a damp squib and fall flat on its face and sink like a stone in water. As for the Gulf War, my heart goes out to not only the the unfortunate Iraqi soldiers who were caught totally unawares by Donald Rumsfeld's "shock and awe tactics" but also the American ones. One cartoon summed it up at the time which showed one American soldier saying to his mate "Pretend to look scary, remember, we are all pretending". It was no different for the Iraqi soldiers. One American soldier hit the nail on the head when he said about Mr.Rumsfeld "he wanted it cheap, he got it". Indeed, politicians the world over don't seem to square up to the realities of war as they send soldiers to fight their wars, wars which nobody wants. And as with the Vietnam war, so with the Gulf War(not to mention Afghanistan) where America used draconian measures like bombs which suck oxygen out of the lungs even as it tried to zero in on documents like 4000 pages of laser enrichment of uranium. Indeed, in global conflicts zones like Afghanistan, the Generals in the Pentagon emerged from the woodwork convinced that there was a goldmine beneath the landmines in Afghanistan. Then there was the thoroughly shabby Kanan Makiya(holed up in Washington) for whom the merciless bombing of his native land was "divine music to my ears". The then Iraqi foreign minister Tariq Aziz, a uniformed sycophant, went verbose with his claims about "shooting American jets like flies". The Iraq War like all wars unleashed the demon in man.

The incumbent Iraqi President is Barham Saleh(his predecessor was Faud Masoom) while the Prime Minister is Mustafa Al Khadimi. Other Prime Ministers include Adil Abdul Mahdi-Al Muntafiki, a Shiaite in Sunni Iraq, an economist who was one of the Vice Presidents from 2005 to 2011, Finance Minister in the Interim government(the government that followed Saddam Hussein) of former Prime Minister Jalal Talabani who passed away a few years back(as of 2019) and Oil Minister from 2014 to 2016. Other Iraqi Oil Ministers include the incumbent Ihsan Ahmed Jaffar Babar etc. Iraq has been led by a succession of Prime Ministers like Haider Al Abaidi, Nouri Al Malki, Ibrahim al Jaafri, Ayad Allawi, Ezzedin Salim, Masood Barzani, Jalal Talabani and others. Iraqi Defense Ministers include the inaugural holder Jafer Al Askari in the erstwhile Kingdom of Iraq. In the Iraqi Republic, the Defense Ministers are Ahmed Zaki, Jafar Baban and others. Defense Ministers in Baathist Iraq include Ayad Allawi, Khairy Rehman etc. Defense Ministers in the present Republic of Iraq include Nouri Al Malki, Saddoun Al Dulaimi, Othman Al Ghnami, Khaled Al Obeidi, Erfan Al Hayali, Najah Al Shammari and the present Inad Juma. Some Shias have quietly ascended the largely Sunni dominated set up of Iraq like Mr. Muntafiki.

Iran

Coming to Shiaite Iran, from which India sources a major portion of its oil(Iran is the world's second largest producer and exporter of oil after Saudi Arabia, but in 2018, it lost the second position to Iraq, that way the world's third largest producer of oil after Iran) supply the Iranian President is Embrahim Raisi who was preceded by Hassan Rouhani under whom the two Vice Presidents were Eshaq Jehangiri and Ali Akbar Salehi(also the Chairman of Iran's Atomic Energy Commission), Ayatollah Khamenei, Ayatollah Ali Khomenei, Mahmoud Ahmedinejad(dubbed an apocalyptic lunatic, America hit the panic button with his ascent) the moderate and liberal Hojatelleslam Ali Akbar Khatami and others. At the time, Ayatollah Ali Khamenei said while Iran faced no immediate threat, he asked the forces to be on alert saying "If America puts its foot in this area, we will cut off that foot." In off and on tensions in the area that have become typical of the Persian Gulf and the Straits of Hormuz, the Straits of Hormuz were ablaze recently(as of 2017) when Iran fired rockets on to ships in the Persian Gulf. Countries like Iran don't seem to respect the sanctity of neutral waters, not that the Persian Gulf is a zone of peace. Iran also sent a drone hustling into Israeli airspace an incident over which the then Israeli PM Benjamin Netanyahu warned the "tyrants in Tehran". But also, on balance, Mr. Netanyahu was effusive in his praise of Iranian King Darius who gave shelter to Jews from Babylon and compared then U.S.President Donald Trump to him and complimented Mr.Trump on his knowledge of Iran. Also, in a security breach, an American RQ170 Sentinel drone fell into Iranian territory while mapping Iranian underground tunnels in Qom and other places and then American National Security Advisor Mr.Tom Donilon said "we are watching Iran's behavior very closely" and speculation was rife that "planes from Moscow and Beijing would be full the next day" an allegory to the possibility of the Russians and the Chinese reverse engineering the drone. A drone is an especially effective way of mapping an area as it can hover over an area for hours on end with no problem. There have been umpteen such incidents in the cauldron that is the Gulf like when Israel struck at the Osirak nuclear reactor in Iraq in a move to pre-empt Iraq from building a nuclear bomb. Foreign Ministers include the incumbent Hossein Amir Abdollahian, who was previously Deputy Foreign Minister for Arab and African Affairs and international affairs advisor to former President Hassan Rouhani who is a former Parliament Speaker. his predecessor Javed Mohammed Zaraf whom then Israeli Prime Minister Benjamin Netanyahu called "the smooth talking mouthpiece of the tyrants in Teheran" and the suave Ali Akbar Velayati and others. Iranian Defense Ministers include the newly appointed General Mohammed Reza Ghareili Ashtiani(a former Vice Chief of armed forces he is sure to up Iran's terror ante), his predecessor Amir Amir Hatami whose commands held included Military Intelligence, the present Interior Minister Gen.Ahmed Vahidi who has been blacklisted by the United States and is wanted by Interpol in connection with the bombing of a Jewish cultural center in Buenos Aires that killed 65 and injured hundreds. Other

Defence Ministers include Ahmed Madani Madani, Taghi Riahi and others. Interior Ministers include as noted earlier Gen. Ahmed Vahidi and others. The incumbent Roads and Urbanisation Minister is former Oil Minister Rostom Ghasemi. The fineprint of this is that this is a hardline cabinet offering a glimpse into the kind of policies that President Raisi is likely to follow in the next four years since his term began in 2021. Iranian Oil Ministers[a key portfolio in oil rich Iran{the rankings of the oil producing nations are as follows:Saudi Arabia, Iran and Iraq}(but in 2018 Iraq edged out Iran to third place)] include the incumbent Javad Owji, his predecessor, Bijan Namdar Zaganeh and others. Born in Kermanshahr in 1952 and educated at the University of Tehran, the distinguished Mr. Zaganeh held several Cabinet posts in his long and distinguished career since the 1979 Iranian Revolution, a cataclysmic event for the world esp. America. The event turned the course of world politics and pushed the Iranian currency, the Riyal and the new Toman, into the doldrums as rapid flight of capital took place from the country with Iran's currency coming up just behind Venezuela's(another oil rich country) Bolivar which tops the charts in terms of the 10 weakest currencies of the world and Iran turned into a "basket" case. Prior to the Iranian Revolution of 1979, an inflection point in world politics and world history, during the American-backed Shah of Persia's time, Iran was called the "West Germany(now Germany) of the Middle East". So also with Iraq, another prosperous country during Saddam Hussein's time. The 8 year old bizarre Iran-Iraq War which started with Iraqi jets striking at targets across Iran plus tyrannical regimes in both countries put paid to any hopes of prosperity in these two troubled countries of the world with both having to scrape the barrel for economic revival. The Iranian Ambassador to the United Nations is the cancer struck Majid Takht Ravinchi, first Ambassador being Nasrollah Entezam. The Iranian mission in New York is, in fact, housed in the Pakistani Embassy. The Iranian Ambassador to India is Ali Chegeni, the inaugural holder being Ali Motamedi. In fact, Mr.Raisi's predecessor, Mr.Hassan Rouhani towards the fag end of his tenure even concluded a doomed nuclear deal with the America-led West. According to reports, Iran has built a nuclear submarine engine, is tapping nuclear energy as a source of electricity, has taken steps towards uranium enrichment and has built centrifuges at its Parchin nuclear facility in moves towards consolidation of its nuclear energy base. Uranium enrichment is the process where uranium gas is passed through centrifuges. The then European Union President Catherine Ashton(present President Donald Tusk) refused to certify that Iran was not manufacturing nuclear fuel at its Parchin nuclear facility a few years ago(as of 2022).

And IAEA Director General Rafael Mariano Grossi, a diplomat with over 36 years of experience in non-proliferation and disarmament is taking a proactive interest in Iran's nuclear moves and brought them under the scanner. Iran, for its part, of course, claims it is a nuclear dove, a claim which flies in the face of evidence to the contrary. As is well known America took out Iranian Revolutionary Guards Commander Qasseim Soleimani and a prominent Iraqi General in a drone strike early 2020. Mr. Soleimani was described as "the architect of Iran's "hand" far beyond the regional architechture and "who should have been killed long back". An example of this is the "role" of Iranian Ambassador to Austria Ebadollah Molaei(not to mention the role of junior mission staff like Minister Hamad Reza Madad and counsellor Mohammed Taghi Ahmed Mohammed) in bombings in France apart from the more well known known incidents. Austria threatened to strip the Iranian diplomat of diplomatic immunity and then proceeded to actually do it also threatened to withdraw its Ambassador to Teheran Dr.Freidrich Stift. However, his successor Stefan Sholz(now Ambassador to China)(Incidentally, Austrian Ambassador to India is Her Excellency Briggete Oppingher Walschofer) called for a "scaling down of the West's threat perception of Iran" as he sought to tamp down on Western "frenzy" about Iran. To buttress this angle of the argument further, Anthony Cordesman, Burke Chair at the Institute for Strategic Studies, Washington D.C. and Michael Knights of the Center for Near East Policy offer these two rejoinders to Western charges about Iran "we tend to demonise these people but they are pretty critical stable figures" and "Mr. Soleimani was promptly replaced by a competent deputy, the Al Quds force Chief Embrahim Qani" and Hossein Salami was made the Director General of the Al Quds force. However, all these can be dismissed as the arguments of a polite lipped Ambassador and the arguments of over enthusiastic academics who are suffering from the "Stockhome Syndrome" who in a way are trying to portray Iran as a paper tiger, and the danger to the world from Iran is real. Out of place here would be not mentioning something about America's Combatting America's Adversaries through Sanctions(CAATSA), a law which is directed against American adversaries like Iran, Russia and North Korea and under which America nearly stopped supplies of Russian S-400 air defense missiles to India(but India stood steady, firm and resolute and now there is even talk of Russia supplying S-500 and S-600 missiles to India with the S-400s already being deployed at a forward Army Base in Punjab near the Pakistan border) but succeeded in scuttling Russian weapons sales to countries like Indonesia with Indonesia dumping Russian Su-35 fighters in favor of American F-16s or French Mirages. But, not so with the Russian Su-57 which Russia supplied to countries like Vietnam and Turkey with India and Russia too thrashing out the Russian Su-57 deal though several roadblocks(or should we say stumbling blocks) are coming up in the deal.

Yemen

The Yemeni Prime Minister is Maen Abdul Malik Saeed but his position is disputed by Mahdi Al Mashat since an inconclusive general election in 2011. This government seated in Aden is the only government recognized by Saudi Arabia and the international community. Among other Prime Ministers is Ahmed Obeid bin-Dagh. Yemeni Presidents include the the first President of unified Yemen Ali Abdullah Saleh who was killed in a successful roadside assassination attempt, Abdrabuh Mansour Hadi and others. Yemeni

Vice Presidents include Abdul Hoti and others. Yemen has been recognized by the United Nations and the international community as a failed state because of its numerous fractious internecine wars, extreme poverty, penury and hunger, spiralling debt(in fact it has fallen into the debt trap), soaring unemployment and numerous other serious problems all seemingly nowhere in sight of a solution.

Jordan

Prime Ministers of the Hashemite Kingdom of Jordan whose King is Abdullah II bin al Hussein(the Queen is Queen Rania) who calls himself "the 42nd descendent of Mohammed"(others Kings are his predecessor King Hussein with his attendant signature American wife and others) include the incumbent Bisher Al Khasawneh, his predecessor Omar Al Razaz, a former Education Minister, Hani Fawzi Al Mulki, Abdullah Ensour, Awn Shaukat Al Khasawneh, Fayez Al Tarawneh, Samir Al Rifai, Nader Al Dahabi, Marouf Al Bakhit, Faisal Fayez, other Prime Ministers include the inaugural holder Rashid Al Talia, Ibrahim Hashem, Abdul Ali Tarawneh and others. Jordan's Deputy Prime Minister and Foreign Minister is Ayman Al Safadi who is preceded by Nasser Judeh and many others.

Palestine

The long suppressed people of Palestine recently at long last got a homeland but just so in the face of continued and stringent Israeli and American instrasigence. Why Israel wags the "dog" America is because of the proactive and powerful Israeli lobby in America, the American Israeli Public Affairs Committee and the large Jewish presence in America. The Palestinian Prime Minister is Dr.Mohammed Shtayyeh(former Prime Ministers include his predecessor Rami Hamdallah, Mahmoud Abbas, Salam Fayad, Manuel Hassassian and others) and the country's two Deputy Prime Ministers are Dr. Zeid Abu Amr who is also the country's Minister of Culture and Dr. Mohammed Mostafa who is the country's Minister of the National Economy. The Cabinet comprises of Finance Minister Shukri Bishara, Foreign Minister Riad Al Malki, Minister of Jerusalem Affars Adnan Al Husseni, Minister of Tourism and Antiquities Mrs Rula Maiaa, Health Minister Jawad Awad, Education Minister Khwala Shakshir, Minister of Telecommunications, IT and Transport Allam Moussa and others. Among the country's Ambassadors to the US are incumbent Ambassador Dr. Riyad H. Mansour, his predecessor Essim Eziekel, Husam Said Zomlot and others. Does the United States recognize Palestine? While the country has recognized Palestine at UNESCO it has not taken any real measures to recognize the Arab country at more appropriate and important forums like the UN, does not have representation in Palestinian territories and does not provide consular services to Palestinians and the country's Ambassador to Israel David Melech Friedman, a political appointee and bankruptcy lawyer, is known for his proactive and notorious interference in Palestinian affairs.

Lebanon

The Prime Minister of Lebanon is as noted earlier Hassan Diab while the President is Michel Aoun. According to the Constitution of Lebanon, the President has to be a Maronite Christian while the Prime Minister has to be a Sunni Muslim. Accordingly, Mr. Aoun is a Maronite Christian while Mr.Diab is a Sunni Muslim. Mr.Diab's predecessor, Saad Hariri(who once went on the record saying that he would probably be assassinated like his father Prime Minister Saad Rafique) again as noted earlier was "abducted" by the powerful Saudi Prince Mohammed bin Salman but the move boomeranged on the Prince and Iran based Houthi rebels who played a key role in Mr.Hariri's release said they stood vindicated.

VIII

Central Asia

Khazakstan

Since Khazakstan broke away from the Soviet Union in 1991 it has had only two Presidents, the powerful former President Nursultan Abishluty or Abesevich Nazarbayev(spouse Dariga Nazarbayeva, daughter Seema Nazarbayeva) whom the incumbent Kassim Jomart Tokayev has jailed. Khazakstan kicked off and rung in 2022 with a crisis. A gas price hike set off and precipitated mass violent protests(such protests are rare in stable Khazakstan). The Cabinet led by Prime Minister Askar Mamin resigned enmass and President Tokayev called for Russian and CSTO(Collective Security Treaty Organisation of which Russia leaning countries like Khazakstan, Belarus etc are members) intervention and and with lightning speed Russia and the pro-Russian security bloc troops, armored columns and electronic warfare systems were deployed and quelled the protests and bought the situation under control. President Tokayev also appointed a new Acting PM Alikhan Smailov.

Uzbekistan

Since it split from the U.S.S.R, Uzbekistan, one among only two doubly landlocked countries(a doubly landlocked country being one where one has to cross two borders to reach the border of the country) of the world, the other being former German colony Leichtenstein which incidentally shares its independence day with that of India, has had only three Presidents, the inaugural holder Islam Karimov whose daughter Gulnara Karimova was sentence to jail by the present government on alleged graft charges, Nino Burjanadze and the incumbent Shavkat Mirzioyev. The Prime Minister is Abdullah Aripov.

Tajikistan

The President of Tajikistan is Khokhir Rasoolzada and the Prime Minister is Emomali Rehman while the Foreign Minister is Sirojuddin Mukhridinovich Aslov who is soon to attend a conference of Central Asian Foreign Ministers hosted by Foreign Minister Dr.Subrahmanyam Jaishankar in New Delhi as part of India's Look West Policy. An ambitious TAPI(Tajikistan-Afghanistan-Pakistan-India) oil pipeline project was envisaged by countries of the region several years back but the condition of India-Pak relations being what it is, the move was a stillborn.

Turkmenistan

Turkmenistan has had only two Presidents since it broke away from the ertwhile U.S.S.R, the incumbent Gurbanguly Muhamedov and Nasirdin Isanov, the first President who died in office whereupon the former took charge. The capital is Ashgabat.

Kyrgyzstan

Prime Ministers of Kyrgyzstan include the incumbent Akylbek Japarov, his predecessor Ulukbek Maripov, Sadyr Japarov, Kubatbek Boronov, Artem Novikov, Muhammedkaly Abulgaziyev, Omurbek

Babanov, Almazbek Atambayev, Sooranbay Jeenbekov, Boris Siluanov, Felix Kulov, the first President Nasirdin Isanov and other glitterati. Presidents include the incumbent Sadyr Japarov, Sooranbay Jeenbekov, Almazbek Atambayev and others. The Presidential Palace is Al Archa Presidential, Bishkek.

Belarus

The President of Belarus is Alexander Lukashenko in office since the former constituent Republic of the U.S.S.R broke away from the U.S.S.R but his position is disputed since September 2019. Prime Ministers include Sergei Lang, Vladimir Yermoshin, Sergei Sidorsky, Andrei Kobyakov, Sairhaj Rumas, the incumbent Roman Alexandrovich Golovko and others.

Azerbaijan

The President of Azerbaijan is Ilham Aliyev with First Lady Mehriban Aliyeva doubling up as the country's Vice President. Other Presidents include the inaugural holder and the present President's father Haider Aliyev and others. Prime Ministers include Novruz Mammadov, Arthur Rasizade, the incumbent Ali Asadov and others.

Armenia

Recently(as of 2021), Azerbaijan and Armenia fought a war and the Armenian Prime Minister is Nikol Paschinyan. The President is Armen Sarkissyan, first President is Levor Ter Petrosyaan, first Vice President is Gagik Harutunyan(the office of Vice President now stands abolished) and 3rd President is Sergh Sarkissyan. The Poverty Data of Armenia are as follows: 26.5% of the population lives below the national poverty line and per capita income is $1.60.

Mongolia

The Mongolian Prime Minister is Luvsannamsrain Oyun-Erdene while his predecessor Ukhnagin Khurelsukh has become the new President as former President Khaltmagin Batulga, a professional wrestler, demits office. Mongolia which used to play little or role in the international arena is fast reaching out to countries like India(for instance, former Minister of State for Defense Pallam Raju visited Ulan Bator to oversee joint military exercises and India and Mongolia conducted other military exercises as well. This reverse "String of Pearls" theory is naturally viewed with concern in Beijing esp. when Mongolia shares a long border(some 6000km) with China, a border which is the second longest in the world next only to the 8,835km American-Canadian border which is the longest in the world.

IX

Australia and Others

Australia

Australia which is part of the anti-China group whose other members are India, Japan and the United States(its other international cooperation is the ANZUS or Australia, New Zealand and United States) security umbrella which includes other American allies has been led by a long retinue of Prime Ministers, 30 in total including one woman. They are as follows: the inaugural holder Sir Edmund Barton(of the Protectionist Party)(MP for New South Wales), George Reid, Chris Watson, Ben Chifley, Joseph Cook, Billy Hughes, Stanley Bruce, Andrew Fisher, Alfred Deakin, William McMohan, Malcom Fraser, Bob Hawke, Frank Ford, John Curtin, John Holt, the Labour Prime Minister James Scullin who appointed Australia's first native Governor General Sir Issac Issacs against the wishes of Britain's King George VI who wanted to appoint Field Marshall Sir Frederick Birdwood, the longest serving Prime Minister Robert Menzies of the United Australia Party, Paul Keating, John Howard, the only woman Prime Minister Julia Gillard, Kevin Rudd, Tony Abbott, Malcolm Turnbull and the present Scott John Sco Mo Morrisson. Australian Governors General include the inaugural holder Capt. John Hope, Earl of Hope Town, the incumbent Sir Edmund Hurley(former Governor of New South Wales), his predecessor Sir Peter Cosgrove, Dame Quentin Bryce, Michael Jeffrey, Bill Hayden, Peter Hollingworth, Sir Issac Issacs and a galaxy of distinguished officeholders.

Australia's Home Minister is Karen Andrew MP who is preceded by Peter Dutton, the Foreign Minister is former Senator Marise Payne who in turn is preceded by Julie Bishop, Alexander Downer and others and while the incumbent Environment Minister is Sussane Ley MP, other office holders include her predecessor Josh Frydenburg, the inaugural holder Sir Peter Howson and in 1997 the Ministry of Environment and Energy was hived off and a separate Energy Ministry was created and put under the charge of incumbent Energy Minister Melissa Price. And important Treasurers include present PM Scott John Morrisson and Josh Frydenburg.

Recent Australian politics has been dogged by shadow boxing which has left the Australian public befuddled, disgusted and aghast. The government of Prime Minister Morrisson is a minority one which has a wafer-thin majority in Parliament as recently the wealthy Wentworth seat has gone to the opposition candidate Kerryn Phleps. However, this was several years back and Prime Minister Morrisson has since consolidated his base in Parliament.

New Zealand

As regards New Zealand, the Prime Minister is Jacinda Ardern of the Labour Party who did a good job of combatting Covid-19 in her country for which she was even nominated for the 2020 Nobel Peace Prize and 2022 she went on record that an outbreak of Covid-19 is inevitable. Former PMs include her predecessor Simon William Bill English(whose children include his son Bartholomew English, his daughter Margaret English and others), Helen Clark(in whose case once the Australian government was left red faced after Australian customs custom checked and frisked her when she was on a visit to Australia), John Key and Sir George Grey, a soldier, diplomat and author who was also Governor of Southern Australia, Governor of Bay Island and who held other important constitutional posts, first Prime Minister Sir Don Kinnock and others. Governors General of New Zealand include the incumbent Patsy Reddy, her predecessor Dame Sian Elias(who served multiple terms including one as Acting G-G), Gen(retd.) Sir Jerry Metparea, Sir Anand Satyanand, Dame Sylia Cartright, Dame Sian Elias, Sir Michael Hardy Boys, Sir Richard Wild, Sir Michael Myers, Sir Robert Stout and scores of others including the first Capt.William Hobson. Deputy Prime Ministers include the incumbent Grant Robertson, Winston Peters who on a visit to India raised Indian hackles by commenting on the Citizensship Amendment Act 2011[passed on December 11, 2019 the CAA 2019 amends the Citizenship Amentment Act 1955 and paves the way for providing Indian citizenship to persecuted minorities from Pakistan, Afghanistan and Bangladesh) claiming people in New Zealand were interested to know,Jim Aderton, Paula Bennet,, John Watt, Horace Wilson, John Wilson, the first Deputy Prime Minister Sir Don Kinnock who went on to become Prime Minister and others. Few studies have been conducted on the office of Deputy Prime Minister but one reliable study by Stephen Bennet lists 5 qualities for a good Deputy Prime Minister:relationship with the Prime Minister, relationship with the públic, public opinion and so on. On this scale, Sir Don Kinnock. and Horace Wilson come up aces while Winston Peters and Jim Aderton end up at the bottom of the heap. Important political parties(esp.for Indians) include the anti-immigrant fringe New Zealand First etc but Prime Minister Ardern's Labor adopts a more tolerant posture towards immigrants.

The Foreign Minister is Naniah Mahuta, a Maori woman while the Minister for Communities, Voluntary Organisations etc is Indian origin Priyanca Radhakrishnan and Gaurav Sharma an MP took his oath of office in Sanskrit. This diaspora diversity in the Cabinet reflects Prime Minister Jacinda Ardern's keeness for providing representation to the various communities, races and the sexes.

Haiti

The Presidents of Haiti since the Haitian Revolution of 1791 are as follows: Haiti declared Independence in 1804. Between 1806 and 1820 Haiti was divided between the Northern Republic renamed Kingdom in 1811 and the Southern Kingdom between 1822 and 1840 during the period known as the Unification of Haiti the President ruled over the entire Island of Hispionola in what is known as Unification of Hispionala. Faustin I, Henri Christophe, Henri I, Jean Pierre Boyer, Francois C.Antoine Simon, Jean Claude Davulier and Francois Davulier of the Davulier Dynasty, Henri Namphy, Henri Saint Leslie Manigat, Pierre Nord Alexis, Raoul Cedras, Council of Secretaries of State, Prosper Avril, Rene Preval, Michel Martelly, Council of Ministers, Jovenel Moise, Council of Ministers Acting Prime Minister Joseph Claude, Council of Ministers Prime Minister Ariel Henry and others.

Fiji

Presidents of Fiji include Penia Ganilau, Mahendra Chaudry, General Sitiveni Liganeni Rabuka, the present President General Jioji Kanousi and others. Prime Ministers include Penia Ganilau, Mahendra Chaudry, the present Prime Minister Commodore Josias Vorque Frank Bainimarama and others. Governor Generals include William Mathew Jackson and others.

Oceania

Mauritius

The Presidents of Mauritius are as follows:Sir Veeraswamy Ringadoo, Angadi Chettiar, Paul Berringer, Monique Ohsan Belepeu, Ameena Gurib Fakim who was involved in a ugly and embarrasing credit card scandal after her credit card bounced after a binge shopping spree and others. The Prime Ministers include Padmashree Sir Anerood Jaugnauth, his son and present Prime Minister Praveen Jaugnauth, Paul Berringer and others. In Mauritius the PM is the power center and the President is only a figurehead.

Madagascar

The Presidents of Madagascar include the incumbent Heir Marshialrakatoarimanana, the inaugural holder Gabriel Rakatoarimananana and others. The Prime Ministers include Olaf Samuelson, Ronald Johnson and others. Defense Minister Rajnath Singh at a meeting of the Indian Ocean Rim Association for Regional Cooperation now Rim Association Defense Ministers had extensive discussions with Madagascar's Defense Minister Richard Rakatoarimanana and expressed India's keeness to develop close military ties with his country in a bid to preempt Chinese expansionism in the Indian Ocean, a matter which is increasingily preoccupying India's attention and of grave concern to India. Madagascar's Ambassador to China Victor Sikonina is the Dean of the Diplomatic Corp. in Beijing.

Samoa

American Ambassadors to Samoa include Judith Ceffkin, Frank William Franklin and others. Indian Ambassador to New Zealand Muktesh Pardeshi resident in Wellington serves as the country's Ambassador to Samoa. The Samoan Ambassador to Washington is Alluiga Fetura Allosiua and the inaugural holder was Maia Vuva Maiua.

Among the island countries of Nauru, Tonga and Tuvalu it is worth noting that Nauru is the only country in the world not to have a capital since its capital is only 2 km in length and American Ambassador to Fiji James Joseph Ceren also serves as the country's

Ambassador to Nauru, Tonga and Tuvalu.

World Political Order-II

Summary

World Political Order II is the second part of a two part series, **World Political Order I** being the first part. In the second part the Writer has handled the world's second largest continent, Africa, a continent whose voice will be heard with increasing frequency, South America, Central America, Carribean and in North America Canada. Which was the most important assassination of the 20th Century and why? What was the big crisis that over took the World midway through the Century which nearly ended the world. Who were the primary movers and shakers in the politics of this part of the world? And more. Read On.....

X
Africa-The Dark Continent

Algeria

Algerian Presidents include the incumbent Abdelmadzid Tebbounne, Abdelaziz Boetflika and others. Prime Ministers include the present academic, Prof.Abdelaziz Djerad, Abdel Malek Sellal and others. Under Article 102 of the Algerian Constitution, in case of the resignation, absence, temporary leave or dismissal of the President, the Vice President becomes the Acting President till such time as a new incumbent is found.

Tunisia

Tunisia Presidents include the first President, the legendry Habib Bourghiba who ruled from 1956-63. After former strongman President Zine El Abidine Ben Ali was forced out by protests led by the dissident Mohammed Bou Azizi(people like Mr. Azizi and Chinese dissident leaders like the 2010 Nobel Peace Lauruate and Joshua Wong are posing a popular challenge to despotic regimes notably China and to a lesser extent Israel) ushering in the Arab Spring which spread like wildfire to other Arab countries, Tunisia has seen a democratic dawn and the National Dialogue Quartet of Tunisia was handed over the 2015 Nobel Peace Prize for scripting democratic history in Tunisia. Other Tunisian Presidents include Beji Caid Essebse, Habib Bourghiba Jr,, Mohammed Ennaceur, the present President Kais Saed and others. Tunisian Prime Ministers include the present Najla Bouden, El Yes Fak Fak, Yossef Chehad, Ahmed Oyaia and others. Foreign Ministers include the incumbent Otman Jerandi, Salma Ennaifer, Noureddine Erray, Sabri Bachtabji, Khemais Jhenaui, Beji Caid Essebse, Habib Bourghiba Jr., Mongi Salim, Habib Bourgibha and others. Defense Ministers include Imed Memmich, Brahim Bartigi, Imed Hazgui, Mohammed El Karim Jhamousi who was also Justice Minister and State Secretary, Abdel Karim Nbidi, Beji Caid Essebse, Habib Bourghiba Jr., Habib Bourghiba and others.

Tanzania

The President of Tanzania is Samia Suluhu Hassan who recently ranted at MPs saying she was "no Magufuli", an allegory to the deceased former President of Tanzania John Magufuli. A respected figure in Tanzania, Mr.Magufuli was, however, a Covid-19 sceptic and he died 2021 suspectedly due to Covid-19. The Prime Minister is Kassim Majaliwa. Former President the leftist leaning Marxist, Julius Nyerere, one of the pillars of the Non-Aligned Movement, wrote a book on Lenin which was dubbed in the West as "a little book on Lenin", a reflection of Darr-es-Salam's leftist leanings, notwithstanding its allegiance to the Non-Aligned Movement which itself was open to the charge from certain quarters of having "leftist leanings".

Somalia

The President of Somalia is Mohommed Abdullahi Farmajo before whom the President was Mohammed Abdul Ali Mohammed and the first President was Abdul Ali Issa during the days of the Trusteeship of Somalia. The Prime Minister is Hassan Ali Khayre. Mogadishu's Minister for Security is Mohammed Abubaker Islow who quelled disturbances in Somalia 2016 with an iron hand.

Ethiopia

The Prime Minister of Ethiopia Nobel Peace Lauraete Abhiy Ahmed Ali who was awarded the 2019 Peace Nobel for his role in ending Ethiopia's long running conflict with neighbouring Eritrea but deliberately the Eritrean President Issais Afwerki or Issais Afewerki was kept out of the prize because of his altercation with a woman. He is preceded by Hailemarian Desalegn(a former Chairman of the Addis Ababa Municipal Corp.) who had to resign following country-wide protests against his misrule. Following this, emergency was imposed in the country announced by Defense Minister Siraj Fegessa Siraj Fegassais following which polls were held and Mr.Abhiy Ali emerged the winner. Before Mr. Desalegn, the Prime Minister was the Marxist rebel Meles Zenawi. The President is Sahle Work Zewde and Mulatu Teshome was the President before her. The incumbent Defense Minister is former PM candidate Lemma Megersa while his predecessor was Motumma Mekessa. While the Finance Minister is Abraham Tekeste the Foreign Minister is former PM and Transport Minister(Mr.Siraj Fegassa is the incumbent Transport Minister) Workneh Gebeyehu(he was dismissed as a choice for PM in the election that saw Mr.Abhiy Ali win as he lacked grassroots support. Ministers of State for Foreign Affairs are Gedu Andargachu and Hirut Zemene(the Agency executive). Other contenders for the PM's post in the election that saw Abhiy Ali win included Deputy Prime Minister in the Desalegn Cabinet Demeke Mekonnen who is hated even more than Abhiy Ali(who was internationally preferred) who his himself a not very popular figure. But because Ali carried the day with the Tigrayans(a minority tribe but politically and otherwise dominant) Peoples Revolutionary Liberation Front(TPRLF), one of the four groups comprising the ruling Ethiopian Peoples Revolutionary Liberation Front(EPRLF) of Mr.Abhiy Ahmed Ali(the other three being Oromo Peoples Democratic Organisation(OPDO) of Mr.Ali, Amhara Peoples Democratic Movement of Mr.Demeke Mekonnen and the Sidamas(whose leader Mr.Shiferaw Shigute of the Southern Ethiopian Peoples Democratic Movement(SPED), a former Education Minister was one of the contenders for the Prime Minister's post), Ali became the Prime Minister. Incidentally, Mr.Ali belongs to the Oromo tribe and Mr.Mekonnen belongs to the Amhara tribe. The Oromos and the Amharas are at loggerheads with each other. Under Mr.Mekonnen's supervision came Ethiopia's giant hydropower dams under the auspíces of the Ethiopia Telecom Authority. There was a fifth PM candidate, Lemma Megarsa of the OPDO who is now the Defense Minister. In fact, the OPDO is known as Lemma's party. After the earlier noted thaw in Ethiopian-Eritrean relations, the Ethiopian President visited Eritrea.

Eritrea

With the creation of Eritrea in 1997, Issais Afwerki or Issais Afewerki took charge as the first and till now only President of Eritrea.

Angola

The first President of Angola was the legendary Marxist rebel Dr.Antonio Augustine Neto, a physician by profession and a poet by choice, who after a long civil war which his Popular Movement for the Liberation of Angola(MPLA) spearheaded became the first President of independent Angola. He died in Moscow in 1976. The First Lady was Eugene Maria Neto and he had a son and daughter, Marie. The second President was Juan Eduardo dos Santos and his wife Ana Paulo Christovao Lemos dos Santos was the First Lady. He was followed by the third and current President Juao Laurenco and the present First Lady is Ana Paulo Juao Laurenco who is the mother of six children, three sons and three daughters. The Vice President of Angola is Bornito de Sousa who is preceded by Manuel Vicenta. The first Prime Minister of Angola was Lopo Fortunato Ferreira do Nascimento(born July 10, 1942) who ruled Angola from 11th November 1974 to 9th December 1978. He was also the Secretary-General of the MPLA.

Mozambique

Mozambique, which has a AK-47 on its flag as the emblem, is headed by President Felipe Nyusi and Vice President Carlos Augustino do Rosario.

Chad

The President of Chad is Idriss Deby and Vice President is Albert Pahimi Phadake.

Central African Republic

The Central African Republic is helmed by President Faustin Archange Touadera and he is assisted in his duties by Vice President Simplice Sarandji. As of 2014, French General Franscisco Soriano was the head of the French forces in the CAR which are fighting rebels seeking to destabilise the country.

Niger

The various Presidents of Niger include the current office holder Mohammed Bazoum, his predecessor Mohammed Issoufou, Salou Djibo, Mamadou Tandja, Dauda Malam Wanke, Mahamane Osmane, Ali Saibou, the first President Himani Diori and others. The Prime Minister is Ouamoudu Mohamadou and he was preceded by Brigi Rafini and others. Mr. Rafini, a ethnic Tuareg belonging to the Iferoune region of Agadez(America's NW African springboard is the Agadez Air Base) and a former Agriculture Minister and 4th Vice President of the National Assembly(Niger's Parliament), he was a PM candidate in every election since 1993. A 9-nation French Barkhane force is involved in anti-terror operations in Niger.

Nigeria

The President of Nigeria is Mahmadu Buhari and the Vice President is Yemi Osinbajo. There were some disturbances in Nigeria's Central Pleateau State 2017. While Libya is the top producer of oil in Africa, oil rich Nigeria too is a major producer of oil and as such is one of the upper income bracket countries of Africa and former Nigerian Oil Minister Mohammed Sanusi Barkindo is currently the OPEC Secretary General. The incumbent Nigerian Oil Minister is Timipre Silva and Mr.Silva's predecessor, the scandal tainted Diezani Alison Madueke was arrested in London and her passport confiscated. Holding about 2.2% of the world's Petroleum reserves, Nigeria ranks 10th in world oil reserves and it is estimated Nigeria has oil reserves 243.3 times its annual oil consumption.

Uganda

Yoweri Musevini is the President of Uganda while Ruhakana Rugunda is the Prime Minister. Uganda seems to be the land of strongmen and dictators like Idi Amin and Milton Obote in the late 80s.

Kenya

This is a country where strongman President Uhuru Kenyatta fortified his position through an election that Chief Justice of Kenya's Supreme Court David Maranga said was "neither free, nor fair". But Kenyatta prevailed effectively neutralizing a challenge offered by his rival Riola Odinga. The ruling African National Union has Odinga Odinga as one of its founders and its ideology is Kenyan nathionalism, conservatism. The Vice President is William Ruto and the former Commonwealth Secretary General Kamlesh Sharma(current Secretary General is Patricia Scotland QC) of India sent former Kenyan Chief Justice Willy Matunga as his Special Envoy to Male, Maldives to mediate in the crisis there some years back.

Egyptian Politics

The peace deal that Anwar Sadat of Egypt signed with Israel's Menachem Begin taking a 180 degree policy turn ended the years of hostility between the two countries but Mr.Sadat paid for it with his life. He was assassinated as he was stepping out of his personal jet on the tarmac of Cairo Airport after his return from a trip aboard. The courageous move on the part of Mr.Sadat was a statesman like act. Perhaps he saw the futility of blindly siding with the Arabs and acted in his country's national interest.Egypt since the peace deal joined Vietnam to some extent in pursuing an independent foreign policy alongwith India and China which have always pursued an independent foreign policy. These four countries escaped all orbits during the cold war and emerged as independent orbits themselves.

Whatever, the current Egyptian President is Abdel Fattah al-Sisi, a former Defense Minister who a few years back won a second term defeating the liberal Ghad party candidate, Abu Mustafa Moussa in an election in which Mr.Sisi was assured of a win and Mr.Moussa posed only a nominal challenge. Mr.Sisi's win was a foregone conlusion. The President of Egypt before Mr.Sisi was Mohammed Morsi who had to put in his papers following country wide violent protests in which hundreds of people were killed and that brought Army tanks on to to Cairo's roads. Mr.Morsi himself dislodged the strongman Hosni Mubarak and former President, the legendary Gamel Abdel Nasser whose nationalisation of the Suez Canal precipitated the Sinai War between Egypt and Israel with British and French jets joining Israel in bombing Egypt. The current Prime Minister is Mustafa Madbouly who is also the country's Minister of Urban Development, Housing and Works. The current Egyptian Defense Minister is Mohammed Ahmed Zaki Mohammed and who is preceded by Sedki Sobhi. The Interior Minister is Mahmoud Tawfik who is preceded in the post by Magdy Abdel Ghaffar. The Civil Aviation Minister is Air Marshal Younes Al Masry who spoke out against the incidents of violence at Cairo airport a few years back(as of 2022). Prior to him, the Civil Aviation Minister was Sherif Fathy. Other famous Egyptians include former UN Secretary General Boutrous-Boutrous Ghali, Arab League Secretary General Abu Moussa and former IAEA Director General Mohammed El Baradei(incumbent is Rafael Mariano Rossi) who shared the 2001 Peace Nobel with the IAEA.

Sudan

Sudan split into Sudan with capital at Khartoum and South Sudan with capital at Juba in 2011 after the Sudanese civil war.

The President of Sudan in the present 18 month transition government(according to Article 19 of the transition constitution the members of the present cabinet are ineligible to run in the election that will follow once the 18 month term of the present government is over. The Sudanese Women's Union protested against this) is Abdallah Hamdok who was nominated for the 2020 Nobel Peace Prize for his role in ushering in democracy and peace in Sudan while the Finance Minister is former Darfur rebel Gibril Ibrahim who was preceded by Hiba Mohammed Ali and Mohammed Elbadawi. The Foreign Ministers include the incumbent Omar Eldin Ismail, Asma Mohammed Abdallah, Ibrahim Ghandour, Ali Ahmed Karti, the inaugural holder Mubarak Zarouk, Keir Ahmed Sati, Ibrahim Ahmed and many, many other distinguished officeholders. The Oil and Energy Minister in oil rich Sudan is Khairy Abdel Rehman who was preceded by Adel Ibrahim and others. The Industries and Trade Minister is Madani Abbas Madani. While Amin El Tom is Minister for Higher Education, Intezar El Soughayroun is the Minister for Education. And the Agriculture Minister is Abdulgadir Turkawi. Lena El Sheik Mahjoub is the Minister for Social Development and Labor. Further, Wala Essam Al Boushi was one of the Ministers for Media, Sports and Youth Affairs. Rashid Talia was the first Justice Minister of Sudan while the present Justice Minister is Nasseredine Boushi. And Yasser Abbas Mohammed Ali is the Minister for Irrigation and Water Resources. And, finally, Yasser Abbas Yasser is the Defense Minister while Gamal Abdul Majeed is the Minister for General Intelligence. And, of course, Al Tairaifi Idriss is the Interior Minister. These are some of the key Cabinet level appointments in the Hamdok government.

The former Sudanese strongman Omar Hassan Ahmed Al Bashir of the National Peoples Congress is undergoing a lenient Correctional Sentence given to him in view of his advancing age. He is 83. The Prime Minister under him was Bakri Hassan Saleh. The contemporary situation in Sudan at that time was such that Sudan, at the time, had three Vice Presidents, the Second Vice President being Hassabu Mohammed Abdal Rehman while present President of South Sudan Salva Kiir Mayardit was also one of the Vice Presidents. Another Vice President was Rashid Bakr.

South Sudan

South Sudan's President is Salva Kiir Mayardit who was Vice President in erstwhile united Sudan and the two Vice Presidents include Taban Deng Gai and James Wani Igga. Ministers include Foreign Minister Beatrice Wanni, Health Minister Akram Ali Altom, Oil Minister Maia Lourent, Minister of Cabinet Affairs Denis Alfred and others.

Libya

The first King of war and strife torn Libya(then a monarchy) was King Idriss I.

After President Muammar Qauddafi, who once said he would waive India's entire oil bill if India shared nuclear secrets with his country, Libya has been ruled by after many heads of state, the National Transitional Council(Presidents Mustafa Abdul Jalil, Mohammed Ali Salim Acting President),General National Congress(Presidents Mohammed Magarief, Guima Ahmed Atiga, Nouri Abu Sahmain), the House of Representatives(Acting President Abu Bakr Baira, Aguila Saleh Issa) and the present Presidential Council(Chairman Fayez Al Siraj who is also the Prime Minister of Libya). After rebels in pick up vans(ably assissted by the United States and the West) stormed the capital Tripoli against the Quaddafi regime a few years back, Libya has been in a political stasis and flux. Uncertainty and instability have been the hallmark of the country. The present President of the House of Representatives is Aguila Saleh Issa and before him was Abu Bakr Baira.

Zimbabwe Politics

Zimbabwe's President is Emmerson Dambudzo Mnangagwa[a former Vice President and Finance Minister(from 1994-1998) under former President Robert Mugabe(at one time the oldest leader in the world and whose wife Grace Mugabe came within touching distance of the President's office in the election that saw Mnangagwa win.) of the Zimbabwe African National Union-Patriotic Front(ZANU-PF) who won the Presidential election defeating Nelson Chamisa. Mnangagwa as a teenager planned a railway track bombing but he was pardoned as he was a minor. Before Mnangagwa, the President was the strongman Robert Mugabe. A much hated figure in the West, Mr.Mugabe ruled Zimbabwe with an iron hand for 40 years before he was ousted in a military coup by Army Chief Gen.Constantino Chiwenga and longstanding intelligence chief Kembo Mohadi. Emmerson

Mnangagwa took over but not before exiled Vice President Phileckezela Phoko returned to Zimbabwe muddying the waters. But, the latter is a spent force and poses no challenge. All in all, Mnangagwa's position seems fortified bringing a degree to the long troubled country. And the leader of the Movement for Decmocratic Change(MDC) Morgan Tsvangirai passed away in a Harare hospital due to cancer.

Mnangagwa has appointed Sibusiso Moyo as his Foreign Minister, the key Agriculture and Farmlands portfolio, a Ministry which at once assumes importance because of the seizure of farmlands from white farmers, has gone to former Air Force Commander Perence Shiri and the Interior Minister is Patrick Chinamasa, a former Finance Minister, with the Finance portfolio going to Mthuli Ncube. Former Finance Ministers include the inaugural holder Nenos Kala, Patrick Chinamasa, Tendai Biti, Ignatius Chombo, Mr.Mnangagwa himself, Obert Pfofu and, of course, the incumbent Mthuli Ncube. The Tourism Ministry which has recently been named as the Tourism, Hospitality, Environment and Ecology Ministry, a ministry rather important in Zimbabwe in view of the tourist potential of the country(for e.g. the iconic Victoria Falls falls in Zimbabwe) has been placed in the hands of Ngobizitha Mangaliso Lovu before whom the Minister was Priscah Mufumira. Incidentally, the former British colony of Rhodesia underwent a bifurcation with Northern Rhodesia becoming Zambia(new President veteran opposition leader Hakainde Hichilema, other Presidents include the first Kenneth Kuanda, Fredrick Chiluba, and the incumbent's predecessor Edgar Lungu and others. The PM is Inonge Wina) and Southern Rhodesia becoming Zimbabwe.

Democratic Republic of Zaire(Congo)

The most famous Congolese politician is the legendary former Congolese President Patrice Lumumba, a pan African and Third World statesman who led the Third World and the Non-aligned

Movement in keeping away from the two power blocs during the Cold War and whose assassination in the early sixties nipped in the bud a budding pan-African and Third World statesman, an assassination which one Belgian author called "the most famous assassination of the 20th century" but what this writer calls the most important assassination of the 20th century as there have been more famous assassinations like the Kennedy assassination but none, perhaps, more important so, as it struck at the very vitals of the Non-Aligned Movement and the Third World, changed the direction and course of world politics, neutralized Third World influence, spurred and fanned further Super Power rivalry and ended the career of a promising statesman. The incumbent Congolese President is Felix Tshisekdi and the Prime Minister is Jean Michel Sana Lukonde. Other Presidents and Prime Ministers include Presidents Joseph Kabila Kabange, Denis Suisso Guesso and others of Democratic Republic Of Zaire(Congo) and Presidents Marien Guoabi and Joachim Yhombi Ophango and others of the erstwhile Republic of Congo and Prime Ministers Sylvester Illunga Illunkamba ,Anatole Collinet Makosso, Clement Mouamba, Alfred Roula, Bruno Tshibala and others of the Democratic Republic of Zaire(Congo)(present day Congo). Vice Presidents include Augustin Matata Ponyo Mopon of present day Congo(Democratic Republic of Zaire) and Aloise Moudileno Massengo, Ange Eduard Poungui, Denis Suisso Guesso, Louis Sylvian Gome and others of the erstwhile Republic of Congo. However, the post of Vice President stands abolished now. Congo, of course, is associated with the Nobel Peace Laureate former UN Secretary General Dag Jalmar Agne Carl Hammarskold(only person to be awarded the coveted prize posthomously) who died in 1961 enroute to the Congo in a plane crash. Incidentally, the media in a sign of haste, reported that Mr.Hammarskold had reached Congo, when, in fact, he had died in the plane crash. In 2018, Congo again was in the news when noted Congolese gynaecological surgeon, Dr.Denis Mukwege of Panzi Hospital, Bukawu, Congo shared the Peace Nobel with Yezedi rights activist Nadia Murad. The good doctor has worked lifelong for victims of sexual violence, many of them requiring correctional surgery.

Ivory Costa(Cote de Iviore)

The President of Cote de Iviore is Alassane Dramane Ouaterra and PMs include the incumbent Patrick Jerome Achi, Hamed Bakayoko, Amadou Gon Coulibaly and others. The Vice President is Daniel Kablan Duncan.

Senegal

The President of Senegal is Macky Sall and the PMs are Abdoul Mbaye, Aminata Toure and Mohammed Abdul Bounne Dionne. Mr. Dionne became the Prime Minister after Christophe Joseph Thabe Kabila resigned with his entire Cabinet prior to which the PM was Aminata Toure.

Sierra Leonne

The first Chief Minister of the Protectorate of Sierra Leonne was Sir Milton.S.Margai and the last was Sir David.J.Francis. The President of present day Sierra Leonne is Julius Maada Bio while Christian Alusine Kamara Taylor, a former Interior Minister was PM 1971-71 and Sorie Ibrahim Karoma, a former Finance Minister was PM 1971-75 and Siaka Stevens held the post from 1975-77. The CM of today's Sierra Leonne is Jacob Jusu Saffa while the Vice President is Mohammed Juldeh Jalloh and his predecessor VP was Daniel Kablan Duncan of the Sierra Leonne Democratic Front.

Ghana

The first President of Ghana was the legendary Kwame Krumah and the country is current headed by President Nana Akufo Addo and his deputy Vice President Mahamudu Bawumia.

Mauritania

The President of Mauritania is Mohammed Ould Ghazouni and the PM is Mohammed Ould Bilal. Other Presidents include the 8th President Sidi Cheikh Ould Abdullahi and Mohammed Ould Abdul Aziz and others. The first PM was Moctar Ould Daddah, also a Speaker of Mauritania's National Assembly or Parliament. Mauritania has twin circulating currencies, the Ouyaia and the Malagasy Ariel which is not divisible by a power of 10.

Seychelles

Seychelles, a country in East Africa, is helmed by President Wavel Ramkalawan whose predecessor was Danny Faure. India transferred a Dornier 228 aircraft for recon missions to Seychelles and undertook to expand its Parliament in sign of growing military and other cooperation between the two countries.

Djibouti

Djibouti in East Africa where China is trying to gain a foothold and has acquired a military base is ruled by President Ismail Omar Guelleh(popularly called IOG). Mr.Guelleh 2017 paid a official visit to China and met Chinese President Xi Jinping and other senior Chinese officials and discussed the expanding China-Djibouti partnership.

Union of the Comoros

Comoros, an archipelago of four islands biggest of which is Mayotte and a former French colony declared its independence from the French in 1974 but Mayotte opted to stay with the French. The UN Security Council condemned this in a resolution and the Union of the Comoros became independent in 1977.

The Presidents of the Union of the Comoros include the incumbent Azali Assoumani, Mohammed Abdullah, Ahmed Abdullah and others. Defense Ministers include Mohammed Ahmed, Mohammed Abdullah and others.

Indian Ambassador to the Union of the Comoros, Abhay Kumar, at 41, is the youngest amongst the current Indian crop of Ambassadors among whom five stand out. Mr.Kumar planted a tree at the University of Antananarivo in 2020.

Botswana

Botswana is led by former PM Mokweesisi Massissi while the Prime Minister is Slumber Tsogwane and the first President was Seretse Khama while the First Lady at that time was Ruth Williams Seretse Khama.

Gabon

The Presidents of Gabon include the incumbent Ali Bongo Ondimba, his predecessor Rose Francine Ragombe, former PM and Vice President Didjob Divungi Di Dinge, Omar Ondimba and Leon Mata. The Vice President is Rose Christian Oussouka Raponda while a former Prime Minister is Pierre Claver Carone who was born on May 8, 1951 in Equatorial Guinea(present day Gabon).

Gabon is a tax haven for the rich to stash away their millions and offers many sops for investors like % capital gains tax and a tax holiday and as such is by African standards, a prosperous country and timber paradise. Recently(as of 2021) in what came to be known as the Kawazzogate scandal there was a scandal involving timber packed in boxes cleared for export. It cost the head of the Minister for Environment, Forests and Ecology and the PM was also in a soup.

Despite its many advantages, Gabon's capital Port Libre is known for its armed robberies, bag snatching and other petty crime and visitors must be careful.

Burkino Faso

Burkino Faso, a small country in Central Africa with capital at Ougagoudou is ruled by its President Roger Kolo and PM Kadre Ouadraogo before whom the Prime Minister was Christian Phillip. Other Presidents include Roch Marc Christian Kabore and others. Mr.Kabore, a banker, was also the President of the National Assembly, or the country's Parliament.

Rawanda

The first President of Rawanda was Pasture Bizimungu and the present President is Paul Kagame while Jeanette Kagame is the First Lady of Rawanda. Louise Mushikiwabo of Rawanda is the Secretary General of the Organization de la Francophonie, the French version of the British Commonwealth, which is responsible for Francophonie relations or promoting French culture and language in former French colonies like Rawanda. Its membership ranges from some of the richest countries in the world like France, Belgium and other countries to some of the poorest like Niger and Rawanda itself and is larger than the British Commonwealth at 46 members to the British Commonwealth's 43.

Burundi

Presidents of Burundi include the incumbent Evarishte Dayishiye, Pierre Kurunziza, Pierre Buyoya of the People's Party and others. Prime Ministers include the incumbent Prosper Bazonbanza etc. Vice Presidents include the incumbent Frederick Bumvginyumvira, Gaston Sindimwo, Joseph Butore, Nickey Yiambo and others.

Namibia

The President of Namibia is Hage Gottfried Geingob and former Finance Minister and President, SWATO Sarah Kugongelwa Amathila is the PM. Walrus Bay, Namibia is known for a particular species of colorful birds which flock there every year.

South Africa

After Nobel Laureate Nelson Mandela picked up the cudgels on behalf of the oppressed people of South Africa under the hated racist regime of President Pik Botha, racism was abolished in South Africa but not before Mr.Mandela served a 27 year prison sentence under racist Mr.Botha. And Mr.Mandela became the first President of post-racist South Africa. He was followed by NKelegelema Mothlantha, Ivy Matsepe Casaburri, Thabo Mbeki and Jacob Zuma who led the African goldmine to world fame through BRICS. Mr.Zuma was followed by the incumbent Cyril Ramaphosa who forestalled a scare by the African National Union President and former Interior and Finance Minister Nkosasana Lamini Zuma to become President. Incidentally, the ANU is a pan African party with presence in countries like Zimbabwe(in alliance with the Patriotic Front), Kenya etc apart from South Africa. South Africa is the only country in the world with three capitals, Pretoria, the political capital, Johannesburg, the judicial capital and Bloemfontaine, the economic capital. Thus, it is a highly decentralized administration.

Lesotho

Lesotho is a small, poor Kingdom in southern Africa which is ruled by King Letsie III(born July 17, 1961) who ascended the throne after the forced exile of his father Moshoeshoe II way back in the 90s.The Queen is Queen Masenate. The Queen Mother is Queen Mother Monmohato Mohato.

The Prime Ministers of Lesotho are as follows:the first Sekhoyana Nehemia Maseribane who was followed by Lebua Jonathan, Mstu Moshele, Pakalitha Moshisili, Hae Fofolo, Thomas

Mothsaehe Thabane under whom the Deputy PM was Manyane Moleleki and who alongwith his wife was arrested on murder charges but later released but the scandal cost him his office and he was followed by the present PM Dr.Moketsi Majoro who is a former Finance Minister and Minister of Natural Resources. Like him, his deputy, Deputy PM Mathibele Makotho is also a former Finance Minister and Minister of Natural Resources.

The Cabinet of Lesotho is as follows:Motlalentoa Letsosa, Home Minister, Prince Maliehe, Defense Minister, Matsepo Ramakoae, Foreign Minister, Chief Thesele Maserebane, Minister for Science and Technology, IT and Telecommunications, Health Minister Matsepo Mokaleto, Agriculture Minister Tefo Mepasela and Minister for Water Resources Nkaku Kabi.

Mali

The Acting President of Mali is Nbah Daw and the Prime Minister is Moctar Ouane who was Foreign Minister in former PM Aminata Toumani Toure's(who passed away 2020 at 76 years) Cabinet. Prior to Mr.Daw, Col.Aissimi Goita, a strongman, deposed then President Ibrahim Bouboucar Keita in a coup.following violent protests that spilled over into the streets. Col Goita declared himself the Chairman of the National Committee for the Salvation of the People but capitulated just 5 days after assuming office under African and international pressure esp. after the West African Economic Treaty Organization imposed sanctions on his regime. The first President of Mali was Modibo Keita. And Secretary General of UN Mission for Mali(MINMUSA) is Mahamet Salahseh Annadif. Still on the same, the French are fighting the Ansar Dine in Mali which has driven the military junta from Northern Mali and is imposing strict Islamic Shariat law there. The French are using Rafale fighter bombers(that India bought) here. Strife torn Mali is also a Malaria testing ground for the Americans and studies on deforestation and loss of pasture land are also being conducted here. The Presidential Palace is the Al Koudibi Presidential Palace, Bamako.

Malawi

The President of Malawi is Lazarus Chakwera and the Vice President is Saulos Klaus Chilima who was preceded by Peter Mutharika. Other Presidents include Bakili Muluzi and Delhi University and Lady Shriram College of Commerce alumni Bingu Wa Mutharika. And Lilongwe is Malawi's capital.

Liberia

The President of Liberia is George Weah, a former football star, who represented Manchester United, Chelsea and other internationally reputed football clubs. Popularly known as "Mister George", he succeeds Ellen Johnson Sirleaf, a Nobel Laureate who shared the 2011 Peace Nobel with two other African women, Lehmah Gbowee and Tawakkol Karman.

Cameroon

Cameroon, a football power, is helmed by President Paul Biya whose son Frances Biya is in the inner clique and is being groomed as a possible successor to Biya Sr. although there are other more worthy candidates some of whom are senior Ministers. The Vice President is Joseph Gute who was preceded by Philemon Yang. The PM post existed until 1962. It now stands abolished.

XI

South America-the Presidential Continent

Mexico

The Mexican elections which saw Andres Manuel Lopez Obrador win, were bloodshed filled elections in which an estimated 300 people were killed with the active participation of drug warlords and drug cartels. Mr.Obrador promised radical changes promising to crack down on Mexico's malaise, drug warlords and drug cartels and has said he will personally storm drug citadels and dens moving about with a skeletal security staff of 10 unarmed men and women as he rings in rapid changes lifting the country out of the morass and stasis which according to Mr.Obrador the outgoing President Enrique Pena Nieto plunged it in.

Mexican Presidents include Francisco Carvajal, Felipe Canales, Luis Videgeray, Gustavo Diaz Ordad, Augusto Mateo Reyes, Felipe Calderon, Vicente Fox, Miguel de la Madrid, Jose Lopez Portillo, Enrique Pena Nieto and of course Mr.Obrador himself.

The Mexican cabinet consists of senior Secretaries or Ministers like Secretary of the Interior(who, given the constitutional implications of the post, is the most important cabinet member and who in case of absolute leave, absence or resignation of the President, takes over as the Acting President. The Secretary is responsible among other things for presentation of bills to Congress, their publication in the Official Journal of the People and the country's primary intelligence agency CISEN is also directly answerable to the Secretary) Olga Sanchez Cordero, Secretary of Finance and Public Credit Arturo Herrera Gutierrez who replaced Carlos Manuel Urzua Macias who resigned sending the Peso tumbling but he was promptly replaced by Mr.Gutierrez, regaining some of the lost ground, Secretary of Foreign Affairs Marcelo Ebrardt who was preceded in the Foreign Office by Luis Videgaray, Secretary of Security Alfonso Durazo, Secretary of Trade Graciela Marquez Colin who was preceded as Trade Secretary by Ildefenso Guajardo of the Institutional Revolutionary Party of President Enrique Pena Nieto. And the NAFTA Negotiator is Jesus Seade. A former Education Secretary is Victor Bravo Ahuja.

Coming to the Secretaries of the Interior(, the various Secretaries of the Interior are as follows:Felipe Canales, Luis Videgaray, Gustavo Diaz Ordad, Franscisco Javier Ramirez Acuna, Juan Camilo Maurino Terrazo, Alphonso Navarette Prida, Miguel Angel Osorio Chong, the incumbent Olga Sanchez Cordero and others.

Coming to the Provincial Governors, the southern Oaxaca State Governor is Alejandro Murat Hinojosa Gobernador who was preceded by Gabino Cue Monteagudo and others. Incidentally, Mr.Gobernador alongwith Interior Secretary Prida survived a chopper crash some years back(as of 2022). Then, the Hidalgo province Governors include Miguel Angel Osorio Chong, Omar Fayyad Meneses and Jose Franscisco Olvera Ruiz. And the Governor of the Free and Sovereign State of Michuacan de Ocampo is elected for a period of 6 years starting Jan 20th and he is not eligible to seek reelection. Some of the Governors include the respected Catemoc Cardenos Solorzano who was also a Federal Deputy and whose loss in the 1988 Presidential election was widely believed to be a case of electoral fraud later conceded by President Miguel de la Madrid. He is one of the most respected figures in Mexican politics, other Governors of Michuacan include Franscisco Javier Ramirez Avina, Gabino Vazquez and the incumbent Silvano Auroeles Cornejo. Mr.Cautemoc Cardenos formed the National Democratic Alternative.

Columbia

Columbia, a country which ranks next only to Netherlands in flower production, has its capital Bogota's Bus Road Transit (BRT) system straight lifted onto New Delhi's streets in the form of Delhi's very own *desi* BRT. But, whereas Bogota's BRT is a huge success, New Delhi's is mired in controversy and failure. Columbian Presidents include the incumbent Ivan Duque Marquez(who while promising business friendly measures, has said he will look at afresh the peace pact that Nobel Peace Laureate Juan Manuel Santos Calderon signed with Columbia's Marxist FARC rebels for which Mr.Calderon was handed over the coveted Peace Nobel. But, so far Mr.Duque seems to have left the deal undisturbed) who promised a thorough overhaul of Columbia's rickety pension system. The Vice President is Marta Lucia Ramirez, a former Defense and Trade Minister. Columbian Presidents include the first the legendary Simon Bolivar Y Palacios who is among the very few to be President of three countries, Columbia, Bolivia and Peru and who commanded the Revolutionary Army before he became President, Rafael Urdaneta Y Faria, Mariano Ospina Peres, Mariano Ospina Gonzalez, Ramon Gonzalez Valencia(also a Vice President), Eduardo Santos(an uncle of Juan Manuel Santos Calderon who ruled Columbia in the 1930s), Jose Augusto Gaviera Trujillo, Andres Pastrana Aranga, Ernesto Samper Pizano, Alvaro Uribe Velez, the Nobel luareate Juan Manuel Santos Calderon, the incumbent Ivan Duque Marquez and others.

Vice Presidents include the incumbent Marta Lucia Ramirez(incidentally Mr.Ivan Duque Marquez and Ms.Ramirez belong to the Liberal Party), General Oscar Naranjo Trujillo, a General in Columbia's National Police and the secret service CEREN, the first Vice President Fransico Antonio Zea Diaz under Simon Bolivar, Angelino Garzon, Domingo de Caycedo Y Sanz de Santa Maria, Franscisco Santos Calderon, Ramon Gonzalez Valencia(2003-2004) and others.

Vice Presidential candidates in the election that saw the Ivan Due-Marta Lucia Ramirez combine win are Juan Carlos Pinzon and Claudia Lopez of the Green Party.

Columbian Defense Ministers include Guillermo Botero Nieto, Oscar Botero Restrepo, Fernando Botero Zea who is the son of prominent painter and sculptor, Manuel Ross, Jose Riva, Rafael Urdaneta Y Faria, Guillermo Prospero whose father was one of the Presidents of Columbia, Marco Aurelio Auli, Minister of War Carlos Soublette, Fernando Londono Y Londono, Ramon Gonzalez Valencia, Ceaser Augusto Gaviera Trujillo, Juan Manuel Santos Calderon, the current Vice President Marta Lucia Ramirez, the incumbent Diego Molano and a long galaxy of glitterati.

The Nobel Laureate Juan Manuel Santos Calderon has said after retirement he will pursue academics and join Amartya Sen's welfare and developmental school and he has been vocal in his criticism of fake news(which the Indian media needs to watch out against) and said he too is a former journalist who owns several media houses in Columbia and knows the pitfalls of fake news. Other Columbian political parties apart from the Liberals include the Conservatives, Columbia First, Center-left, Center-right, Centrists and other parties.

XII
Central America

Nicargua

The leftist Sadinista regime in Nicargua is headed by Mr.Daniel Ortega whom the CIA has tried to dislodge, even assassinate including a military intervention in the 80s and 90s, but, Mr.Ortega like Mr.Castro in Cuba has proved to be a cat with nine lives and after more than 20 years of rule is still in saddle. But the Sadinistas(whose legendary leader led the Sadinista movement way back in the 19th century and again in the 1970s to dislodge the American backed government in Managua) have turned Nicargua into a basket case but it is clear that Mr.Ortega will remain in office as there is no serious opposition to his rule. As one leaves Managua airport, one sees the after effects of his misrule as amidst cars lining the road, there is widescale poverty, a typical scene in a Third World country. The Vice President of Nicargua is Moses Omar Helleslevens Acevedo.

Honduras

In 2017, the people of Honduras elected incumbent President Juan Orlando Hernandez to a second term as even as Xiomara Castro, the first female President of Honduras followed him in that job. 1st Vice President Ricardo Antonio Alvares Aries(a former Mayor of Tegucigalpa) gave way to Vice President Jose Gabriel Garcia. In fact, Honduras has three Vice Presidents, Mr.Garcia being the 1st Vice President. However, President Manuel Zelaya has since abolished that post.

Panama

The President of Panama is Juan Carlos Varela while Vice Presidents include Isabel Saint Malo and others.

Guatemala

Presidents of Guatemala include Alejandro Giammattei, his predecessor Jimmy Morales, Alvaro Torres who wife Sandra Julieta Torres Casanova was a presidential candidate in general elections 2015 and 2018 apart from being First Lady of Guatamela during Mr.Torres's presidency in 2011.

Costa Rica

The President of Costa Rica is Carlos Alvarado Quesada preceded by Luis Guillermo Solis while Epsy Campbell Barr(born July 4th, 1964), the first black woman to hold the job, is the 1st Vice President who was preceded by Ana Helena Chacon Echeverria and Marvin Rodriguez Cordero who is preceded by Helio Fellas is the 2nd Vice President.

El Salvador

El Salvador, the smallest Latin American country, 2021 became the first country in the world to adopt the virtual currency Bitcoin as its official currency and is helmed by its President Nayib Armand Bukele Ortiz who is preceded by Salvador Sanchez Ceren. The Vice

President is Oscar Ortiz.

Brazil

After the sentencing of former President Workers Party's Luiz Inacio Lula da Silva to a 12 year jail sentence for alleged graft(Federal Court Judge Og Fernandez and Appeals Court Judge Jauo Pedro Gerbran Neto sentenced him sentenced him, but not before Federal Court Judge Sergio Moro released him only for the decision to be overturned by Mr.Neto) Brazil elected the present president Jair Messias Bolsonaro(a former police captain and Sao Paulo Mayor) who promised a raft of economic reforms seen as crucial to jumpstart an ailing economy and also won the vote on a platform of cleaning up the political and economic system and the country of crime lords who defeated around 13 candidates(during which some rebel partymen of Mr.Bolsonaro's party protested before the Election Commission about possible electoral fraud) led by Mr.Ferdinando Hadad in a run off securing 55.1% of the vote to Mr.Haddad's 46% to become President. Mr.Bolsonaro is from the same party as Mr.Lula Silva and may have benefited from the latter's vote share. Incidentally, Mr.Bolsonaro was Vice President under Mr.Lula Silva. He takes over from Mr.Michel Temer who in turn took charge from Ms.Dilma Roussef before whom Lula Silva was head of State and head of government.

Paraguay

Paraguay's President is Mario Abdo Benitez and the Vice President is Hugo Velazquez who succeeds Alicia Puchota who in turn succeeds Juan Afara. The first Vice President was Mariano Gonzalez. Mr.Benitez took charge from Horacio Cartes.

Uruguay

The Presidents of Uruguay include the incumbent Louis Lacalle Pou who is the son of former President Louis Alberto Lacalle Herrera. Other Presidents include Tabare Vazquez and Alvaro Torra who is the poorest former President of a country and 2021 Uruguay also rung in a new Vice President, Lucia Topolansky giving way to Beatrice Agrimon.

Ecuador

Ecuadorian Presidents include the incumbent Lenin Moreno, Alvaro Garcia, Emilio Eguinaldo Y Herrera, Osvaldo Hurtado, Jose Joao Pedro Gutierrez, Javier Gonzalez and others. Ecuadorian and Chile football mania is so much that once the two countries went to war over a football match.

Bolivia

Bolivian Presidents include the "first" Simon Bolivar Y Palacios regarding whom and Andres Manuel Garcia there is a dispute as to who was the first President of Bolivia. While Simon Bolivar, the President of three countries Bolivia, Columbia and Peru took oath of office on August 1, 1822 is regarded by some as the first President of Columbia others regard Garcia who entered office on August 11,1822 as the first President only for Bolivar to come back via the back door. However, for all practical purposes, President Andres Manuel Garcia is regarded as the first President of Bolivia.

Other Presidents include German Bass who died in office, Pedro Suico who was assassinated, at 40, the youngest President Antonio Andres Manuel Suico, 2 women Presidents, Jose Pedro Gutierrez, Javier Manuel Pando, Luis Gonzalo Y Gonzalo, Ferdinand Maddad, Alvaro Garcia Linera, Carlos Pucheta, Herrera Plaza, the cocalero activist, the immensely popular Evo Morales Ayma who was persuaded by the small but wealthy groups of Santa Cruz backed by Commander-in-Çhief William Kaliman to step down in favor of the obsure and autocratic Senator belonging to the opposition Social Demoocratic Movement who barred Morales from contesting in future elections and who used Covid as a pretext to postpone elections which were held after all in which Mr.Morales's protege the present President Louis Arce took office but not before Mr.Morales imposed upon himself an exile from which he returned following which Mr.Arce got elected. Former Vice Presidents Alvaro Garcia Linera and Carlos Plaza are Presidential candidates as well Carlos Plaza in the election which saw Arce becoming President and once in 2002. Other Presidential candidates include a conservative South Korean Evangelical Pastor who did surprisingly well securing 8% of the vote but may be that's not so surprising after all considering the conservative disposition of the Bolivian people.

Venezuela

Venezuela's President is Nicholas Maduro but his status is disputed by jailed opposition leader Juan Guaido who is recognized by most of the America led West but some countries notably Turkey, Iran and North Korea recognize Mr.Maduro to be the legitimate representative of the Venezuelan people. Hugo Chavez was the President before Mr.Maduro. Mr.Maduro 2016 charged neighbouring countries like Columbia of instigating the immigrant Venezuelan population against him and sabotaging his government. Oil rich Venezuela is a key oil producing and exporting country and the Venezuelan Oil Minister is Tareck Zaidan El Aissimi Maddah.

Chile

Chile(which at 2% has one of the slowest growth rates in Latin America) 2022 elected a new President Gabrielle Boric. Other Presidents include the first Juan Manuel Encalada, Augustin Ezyaguirre, Ramon Friere Serrano, Fransisco Antonio Pinto the incumbent's predecessor Juan Manuel Sebastian Pinera Echenique who like so many politicians around the world, had pan-party loyalties across the political spectrum at different points of time, parties which include Peruvian for Change, Independent, Peru Vamos etc., Michelle Bachellet who is now the UN High Commissioner for Human Rights with her office in Geneva.

Peru

After the strongman Alberto Fujimori(who came to power in a coup and who once dismissed Western assistance as "insufficient" much to the irritation of Western countries) demitted office Peru has seen a succession of governments led by Presidents such as Pedro Pablo Kuczynski who pardoned Fujimori in return for a reprieve by the latter's lawyer son Kenji, Merino Manuel De la Lama, Martin Alberto Vizcarra Conejo, the engineer from Penn State University and alumini of Catholic Pontifical University of Peru Rafael Sagazier Hochausler OSP who was a development economist with the World Bank apart from holding several important jobs like the one with UNCTAD etc. in his long and distinguished career spanning 37 years, the incumbent Pedro Castillo. The Health Minister is Hernando Carvello.

Other Presidents include the first Simon Bolivar Y Palacias, the great Argentinian General Jose Francisco de San Martin Y Motorras of Argentina, Chile, and Peru who liberated the Central and Southern parts of South America from the Spanish Empire who is also known as the Protector of Peru and died in France in 1850, Jose de la Riva Aguero, Ramon Castilla, Jose Pedro, Fernando Hernandez, Arnaldo Tamayo Mendez, Fernando Lombardi, Alan Ludwig Gabriel Garcia Peres and others.

Prime Ministers include Fernando Hernandez, Jose Pedro, Ramon Castilla, UN Secretary General Javier Peres de Cueller, Vicente Zeballos, Cesaer Villaneuva, Mercedes Rosalba Aaros Fernandez, Violetta Bermudez, the incumbent Mirtha Vazquez and others.

Vice Presidents include Second Vice President Mercedes Rosalba Aaros Fernandez(born August 5th, 1961), an economist and professor who was the country's representative at the Inter-American Development Bank. Ms.Fernandez who studied at the University of Miami, University of the Pacific, and Miami Business School took charge on March 23, 2018 but she has since demitted office and the post is currently vacant. She also served as the country's PM from September 17, 2017 to April 2, 2018. Mr.Vizcarra also served as the First Vice President before taking over as the President.

The Ministry of Foreign Relations or Ministry of Foreign Affairs of Peru is responsible for the conduct of the external relations of Peru and attends to and accredits foreign ambassadors and consuls or international organizations with seat in Lima. It is responsible for bilateral affairs, multilateral affairs and consular affairs of Peru.

Foreign Ministers include Jose de la Rio, Signeur de Sussy, Ramon Castilla, Jose Espina Reyes, Manuel Ross, Juan Jose Antonio Belaunde, Elizabeth Astete Rodriguez, Nestor Popolio Bardellas during the tenure of President Alan Gabriel Ludwig Garcia Peres and who was sacked following his controversial comments on Covid-19 giving way to the incumbent Alan Garcia and others.

Culture Ministers include the actor, lawyer and film star and PM Salvador Jorge Del Solar Labarthe during the tenure of PMs Caesar Villaneuva and Vicente Zeballos and Jorge Nieto Montesinos and Alejandro Neyra Sanchez during the presidency of Fernando Lombardi. The Presidential Palace is in Lima.

Argentina

Argentinian Presidents include the incumbent Alberto Fernandez, his predecessor Mauricio Macri, Christina Martinez de Kirchner, her husband Nestor Kirchner, the legendary Juan Peron[former 4 time Governor of Santa Fe(1992-98)(1998-2002)(2002-2006)and(2008-2012)] and others.

Vice Presidents include the current Christina Fernandez de Kirchner, her predecessor Marta Gabriella Michetti, Isabel

Martinez de Peron, Alejandro Gomez, Issac Rojas, Juan Pistarini, Juan Domingo Peron, Ramon Castillo, Julio Argentino Pascual Roca, Enrique Santamarina, Enrique Martinez and others. The political elite of Argentina is, of course, led by the legendry Perons and the Kirchners.

Mention of Argentina without reference to the 1982 Falklands(Malvinas Islands for the Argentinians) War is incomplete. The outcome of the War was a foregone conclusion(Britain won it) but not before Argentina sent Condor and Exocet missiles hurtling on to British ships. Incidentally, the former British Chief of Naval Staff, Admiral Phillip "Phil" Andrew Jones commandeered the H.M.S.Beaver during the war.

Carribean

Cuba

The President of Cuba is 59 year old Miguel Mario Diaz-Canel Bermudez who is a a former First Vice President and an Electrical Engineer who is preceded by Mr.Fidel Castro's son, Raul Castro(himself a former Vice President) who in turn is preceded by the 'cat with nine lives' like Nicargua's leftist President Daniel Ortega, the legendry revolutionary Fidel Castro who reportedly survived around according to one estimate 620 assassination attempts by the CIA, who was at the helm for 52 years (from 1959-2011) becoming in the process the longest serving Head of State or Head of Government in the world and who during his visit to India had the press eating out of his hands asking for India's steel production, coal production etc. Before Castro, the American backed dictator Fulgencio Batista ruled Cuba but he was deposed in the 1959 world famous Communist Cuban Revolution personally spearheaded by Mr.Castro and his band of young revolutionaries. Indeed, until the collapse of the Soviet Union in 1991, poverty in the Third World seemed fertile breeding ground for left wing extremism much of it fanned not in the least measure by the Soviet Union whom as is well known Ronald Reagan once in a moment of exasperation with the former's allegedly "devious tactics" called "an empire of evil" and cartoonists taking a cue had a field day. Then, of course, John Foster Dulles sanctimoniously dismissed the Non-Aligned Movement as "immoral".

The 1976 Cuban constitution provides for several Vice Presidents the current ones being-1st Vice President Salvador Valdes Mesa, 2nd Vice President Ramiro Valdez Menendez, 3rd Vice President Roberto Tomas Morales Ojeda, 4th Vice President Gladys Maria Lopez Portillo, 5th Vice President Ines Maria Chapman and 6th Vice President Beatrice Johnson.

Former Vice Presidents include Miguel Mario Diaz Canel Bermudez, Jose Ramon Machado Ventura, Raul Castro and others.

The year 1962 was a key year in Cuba's history when first, President Kennedy ordered the Bay of Pigs invasion which fell flat on its face and for the Americans in the words of the President "the shit hit the fan" and "the President of United States is the most lousy job in the world. You can have it Lyndon once I am through".

Secondly, the wily fox the Soviet President Nikita Sergei Krushcev sensing the Soviet lack of ICBMs placed nuclear tipped missiles right at America's doorstep, in Cuba. President Kennedy reacted forthwith with courage and threatened nuclear annihilation if the Soviet Union did not remove the missiles within 24 hours. Fortunately, better sense prevailed and President Krushcev showing statesmanship(chickened out is more like it) removed the missiles. Interestingly, during the entire episode, the Americans deliberately let out their movements, the shipment of missiles, troop and truck movements etc to the Russians since nuclear war is MAD(Mutually Assured Destruction). The Chinese reaction during the episode was also interesting. Peking's Ambassador to Cuba during the Cuban missile crisis, Wu Lengxi, when asked of Krushcev move said "Of course, we did not support Krushcev's move, but we did not oppose it." It is said a diplomat is a man who to hurl a stone, says nice doggie. So also the Ambassador's statement is a nuanced statement. By leaving out the word "either" at the end of the statement, the Ambassador toned down China opposition to Moscow's move.

And vast military industrial complexes in the Super Powers and the smaller regional satraps have always fuelled endless militancy and war which alongwith neo-liberal and other retrosexual policies in the words of noted public intellectual Noam Chomsky "led to a very, very marginal decline in lifespan in the United States from 78.1 years to 78 years". This seems to be further borne out from the fact that small countries like Sweden, Norway and Switzerland which have long since given up the urge to retain empires and have studiously shunned war and kept it at bay seem to enjoy longer average lifespans. For e.g. it is 82 for women and 80 for men in Norway. And in our country, India, it is 65. However, the United States leads the world in the number of centeneranians followed by Japan with 700. Much of it is due to improved health facilities and like factors.

Under the 1976 Constitution, the President is officially called the President of the Council of State and the inaugural holder is Fidel Castro and the Vice President is known as the Vice President of the Council of State. The Appointer of the President is the National Assembly of Peoples Power and the Presidential Palace is the Palacio de la Revolucion. The President can be appointed for a term of 5 years, renewable once. The Cuban seat of power in Havana, the Capitol, resembles its American counterpart. But, that's where all the resemblance ends. Cuba has for long been a Communist bastion right at the doorstep of the citadel of Capitalism. The contrast couldn't be more.

Only now Cuba in the throes of a severe economic depression and slump caused by years of economic mismanagement, lack of reforms and retrograde economic policies is reaching out to America. President Bermudez has his task cut out for him. However on balance, Cuba, one of the world's few centrally planned economies has one of the world's best healthcare systems and was better off economically when it was on Soviet crutches and the

Soviet Union used to bail it out and it was on Soviet life support.

However, gone are those days, the year is 2022 not 1962 and Cubans like it or not have to live with the Americans as much of the world is doing. Besides, the Americans are their neighbours and as the old saying goes we can choose our friends but not our neighbours.

In 2011 after more than half a century of mutual distrust and hostility, Cuba and America established diplomatic relations and President Obama visited Cuba. With American assistance, the Cuban economy is slowly limping back to normalcy. Cuba has twin circulating currencies, the peso and the convertible peso pegged to the U.S.Dollar. The more than 3.3 million Cubans employed in public sector undertakings are dependent on the peso. The Cuban economy's plus points include a thriving tourism sector and the more than $3 billion sent in remittances by overseas Cubans. An example of Cuban-American cooperation is America is importing Cuban cigars and wines and American tourists are flocking Cuba boosting the buoyant Cuban tourism industry. America also recently declassified the Kennedy era files.

Jamaica

Presidents of Jamaica include the first the legendry Hero of Jamaica William Alexander Clarke Bustamante GBE PC who is revered in Jamaica and who founded the Jamaican Labor Party after the labor riots of 1936 and who also founded the Bustamante Industrial Trade Union besides being the first Chief Minister(1962 after Jamaica gained independence from Britain), P.J. Patterson, Portia Simpson Miller(born 1973, age 49 years) ON, Bruce Golding, the incumbent Andrew Michael Holness ON MP, Michael Manley who by far is the most popular President, Edward Leake, Christopher Tufton, Norman Manley and others. Governors General include Christropher Clifford, William Blackburn and others. Some of the other CMs include Bob Davis and others.

Bahamas

PMs of Bahamas include the incumbent Hubert Alexander Minnis, Perry Gladstone Christie, Lyndon Pindling(Commonwealth of Bahamas), Sir Roland Symonette(1969-1971)(CM-1965-1969). The Permanent Secretary of the Bahamas is Jack Thomson and the Parliamentary Secretary is Jeremy Thompson.

Trinidad and Tobago

PMs of Trinidad and Tobago include the incumbent Keith Christopher Rowley, Kamla Prasad Bissessar, Patrick Manning, Basdeo Pandey, the first Elis Clarke and others. Presidents include Paula Mae Weeks, Anthony Carmona, George Maxwell Richards, A.N.R.Robinson, the first Eric Williams and others. Ministers include Allison West, Minister for Urban Development and Housing, Maxie Cuffie, Minister for Public Information and Minister of Health Terrence Dayalsingh. The Mayor of Port of Spain, the capital, is Joel Martinez. The then Indian Ambassador(incumbent Arup Sen) toTrinidad and Tobago Bishwadip Ray held wide ranging discussions with Miss Maxie Cuffie, Terrence Dayalsingh and Mr.Joel Martinez. Trinidad and Tobago has a large Indian diaspora most of whom came as indentured labor and fittingly enough, the national dress for women, at least, is the Sari.

Dominica

Presidents of Dominica include the first Sir Louis Cools Lartigue, Nicholas Green, Eluid Williams, the incumbent Charles Angelo Savarin D.A.H and others.

Dominican Republic

Presidents of Dominican Republic include the incumbent Louis Abinader, his predecessor Danilo Medina, Margarita Lizardo de Ferdinandez better known as Margarita Cedeno De Ferdinandez and others. The PM is Roosevelt Skeritt, MP for Vielle Case constituency since 2010.

Papua New Guinea

The Governor General of Papua New Guinea, an island chain in the South Pacific, is Bob Dadae. Presidents include Sir Julius Chan, Bill Nelson, Peter O'Niel, Sir Michael Marauta, Michael Somare, Sir Rabie Namallu, John Galvin, Sam Abal, the incumbent President James Maraepe and others.

Guinea

The PM of Guinea is Moses Veeraswamy Nagamuttoo.

Barbados

The PM of Barbados is Mia Amor Mottley who is preceded by Freundel Jerome Stuart PC QC MP.

Grenada

The PM of Grenada is Keith Christopher Mitchell who is into his fourth term. Any discussion of Grenada will be incomplete without mention of the infamous American invasion of Grenada during the late 1980s.

Suriname

The President of Suriname is Chen Santokhi who is preceded by the Indian origin(Bhojpuri Bihari) Desi Bouterse. The incumbent Foreign Minister is Albert Ramchand Ramdin(born August 8th, 1952) who is preceded by Yildiz Pollack Bighle during Bouterse's time. The Vice President is Ronnie Brunswick. There is a large Indian and Chinese diaspora in Suriname as is the case with much of the Carribean. Many of them came as indentured labor and later made good.

Antigua and Barbuda

The PM, Finance Minister, Minister for Corporate Governance and Public Private Partnership(PPP) of Antigua and Barbuda, an island country in the Carribean is Gaston Alfonso Browne(born Feb 9th, 1967). Other PMs include the inaugural holder Vere Bird, Lester Bird in whose Cabinet Robin Yearwood was Deputy PM, Finance Minister, Minister for Agriculture, Land and Fisheries, Minister for Aviation, Public Information and Public Utilities at different times and others. Leaders of Opposition include Lester Bird, Robin Yearwood, Benjamin Stedroy and others.

Solomon Islands

The PM of Solomon Islands is Manasseh Damukana Sogavare, a former member of the Congress of Deputies.

St.Kitts and Gerandine

The President of St.Kitts and Gerandine is Ralph Gonsalves.

XIII
North America

Canada

The PM of Canada is Justin Pierre James Trudeau PC MP(who is the second youngest PM after Joe Clark) who ended 8 years of Conservative rule led by PM Stephen Harper PC, other PMs include Paul Martin, Jean Chretien, Kim Campbell, Brian Mulroney, John Turner, Pierre Trudeau whose son died in an avalanche and grief stricken father died within a year perhaps of shock, Joe Clark, Pierre Trudeau, the giant Lestor.B.Pearson, John Diefenbaker, Louis St.Laurent, the legend William Lyons MacKenzie King and others.

The titular head and Head of State of Canada(and Australia) the British Queen, is assisted in her duties by the Governor General of Canada, currently Julie Payette who is preceded by David Johnston, Michelle Jean who in a quirk of fate(both British and French connection) headed the French Commonwealth, the Organisation Internationales de la Francophonie which is responsible for Francophonie relations in former French Colonies like Canada(Canada has a French quarter not to speak of being a former British colony so perhaps Miss Jean's dual responsibilities do add up) or promoting French culture and language in former French colonies. The first Governor General was the Viscount Monc.

The Foreign Minister of Canada is Christina Alexandra 'Christia' Freeland PC MP who is preceded by Stephanie Dion. The first Sikh Defense Minister of Canada was Sajjan Singh. And the Health Minister who was recently in the news in the context of Covid-19 is Jean Yves Duclos.

The Provinces

Nova Scotia

Nova Scotia's Premier is Stephen McNiel, other Premiers include Phillip Carthill and others. Lt.Governors include the incumbent Arthur Johnson, Kathleen Wayne and others.

Ontario

The Premier or Governor of Ontario is Douglas "Doug" Ford, other Governors include his predecessor Elizabeth Dowdeswell, Paul Newman, Alexander Key and others. Recently, Ontario's Minister of International Trade Michael Chan held wide ranging discussions with Chinese Foreign Minister Wang Yi on Chinese investment and trade in Ontario.

Milton Keynes UK
Ingram Content Group UK Ltd.
UKHW011120180424
441376UK00004B/104